£1

BUMF

BUMF

Alan Coren

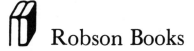 Robson Books

The author would like to thank the proprietors of Punch *magazine for permission to reproduce material in this book.*

FIRST PUBLISHED IN GREAT BRITAIN IN 1984
BY ROBSON BOOKS LTD., BOLSOVER HOUSE,
5-6 CLIPSTONE STREET, LONDON W1P 7EB.
COPYRIGHT © 1984 ALAN COREN.

British Library Cataloguing in Publication Data
Coren, Alan
   Bumf
   I. Title
   828/.91407   PR6053.067/

ISBN 0-86051-291-6

Printed in Hungary

Contents

Thought for Today

I once went, during a recent spell as international businessman, to Finland in order to discuss the purchase of paper; which is, as you know, the country's second largest export, after rally drivers.

At one stage of our discussions, my host, on whom anonymity is perforce conferred through no fault of either of us (it is simply that his name, being made up of eight k's and five m's, is the same as everybody else's there), asked whether I should like to visit a fir plantation, to see books, as it were, on the hoof.

This opportunity I snatched at eagerly, there being nothing else on in Finland at the time apart from a hotel video of *The Lavender Hill Mob* apparently dubbed by tree frogs with no adenoids, and was thus Saabed across several hoursworth of englaciated ruts to a vast gelid tract, equidistant from Pokka and Lokka, on which grew a million-odd trees.

We disembarked into a morning where the breath fell in broken fragments from the lip, and strode Finnishly into the serried trunkwork; whereupon my host launched into vivid chatter about pulp and processing, in perfect English but no less incomprehensible for that.

As the director of a magazine publishing company with at least notional power of attorney, I felt it incumbent upon me to show some professional interest, and perhaps even a little expertise, since negotiations had not yet reached the fine-tuning stage, and big bucks were about to be involved.

I struck a tree with my briefcase.

'Is this to be one of ours?' I said, brightly.

He laughed for perhaps two minutes. His head disappeared in a cloud of expelled hysteria. Clearly, Finns have either a wonderful sense of humour, or none.

'*This?*' he gasped, finally, '*this?* This is not for magazines, *this* is for, kof, kof, kof, lavatory paper!'

I chuckled good-naturedly; as, caught out, any prat will.

'I see,' I said. 'Is there a big difference, then?'

He looked at me, his face recomposed to Arctic gravity.

'Oh, yes,' he said. 'This is much more valuable.'

I have thought about that reply many times since. It may have been, of course, simply the tiniest and most forgivable mistranslation: he may have meant only that it was more expensive.

But how can I be sure?

AC

Birds of a Feather

FRED the usually talkative parrot hasn't said a word since burglars stole £40,000 worth of china and cutlery from under his beak at his owner's shop in Banbury, Oxon. A detective said : " If only he would give us a name . . . he must have heard the men calling to one another."

Daily Express

SHACKLED BY a fine gold 18-carat chain, possibly Indian, the hasp amusingly fashioned to simulate a python eating its own tail, *circa* 1850, to a rare and interesting mottled-green Ferrara marble column, believed to be early seventeenth century, some restoration to base, the shaft fluted and the capital pleasingly decorated with a typical flourish of acanthus leaves, formerly the property of a gentleman, the parrot glared out at the chill November sleet slanting down from the Banbury nimbus, and swore silently to itself.

The Marquesas Islands, thought the parrot, rolling the magic syllables noiselessly on its black and bulbous tongue, the Marianas; Pitcairn, Guam, Tuamotu. Somewhere east of Raratonga, where the best was like the worst, that was the place for a parrot, perched on a mildewed epaulette beside a rum-reeking beard, guarding the blind side of its terrible owner's monocular face against treachery. A parrot should feel the burning Solomons sun on its feathers, a parrot's wrinkled eyes should squint against the glinting South Pacific spume thrown up and rainbowed by the coral reefs. It should smell salt and pemmican and black powder and limes, it should nibble weevils tapped from its master's biscuit.

'Pieces of eight!' shrieked the parrot suddenly, involuntarily; and in the empty elegance of the shop, a dozen crystal chandeliers shook nervously and sent back the splintered light.

The shop-bell tinkled, and two slim young men shimmered in. They began to touch the *objets*—an ivory lorgnette-case, a shrivelled Netsuke, a chipped Delft posset-pot—with long delicate fingers.

The parrot fixed a terrible red-veined eye on them.

9

'Shop!' it screamed.

The young men looked up, startled.

'Oooh!' cried the taller of the two, 'she *talks!*'

The parrot ground its beak. Tiny shards flaked off.

'Fred,' said the parrot, 'is the name.'

'*Fred!*' exclaimed the tall young man. 'He says he's called Fred! Isn't that a wonderful name, Adrian?'

'Very husky,' said the smaller young man. 'I've come over all goose-bumps, Derek.' He took a small neat step towards the parrot. 'Who's a pretty boy then, Fred?'

There's no answer to that, thought the parrot.

The owner of the shop hurried in from the rear office, on a wave of Aramis Pour Lui, smiling.

'May I be of any assistance?' he said.

He ought to have a wooden leg, thought the parrot bitterly, he ought to have scurvy. One ear.

'*May I be of any assistance?*' it cackled, vainly attempting to purse its beak. '*May I be of any assistance?*'

Adrian clapped his pale hands.

'Isn't he *loyal!*' he cried.

'Devoted,' said the owner.

The parrot stared out of the window. Its tightened claws scored the green marble.

'Can I give him a Smartie?' said Derek, fishing in his moleskin bolero. 'Would he take it from my mouth?'

Bloody try it, thought Fred, bloody try it, that's all.

'It mightn't be wise,' said the owner. 'They're one-man pets.'

'We know the feeling,' said Derek, 'don't we, Adrian?'

They shrieked.

'Seriously, though,' said Derek, 'me and my friend Adrian were looking for a Tiffany lamp for our wine-table.'

'We don't use it for wine, though, do we, Derek?' said Adrian. 'We use it to display our *objets trouvés*. We go to Southwold every year—'

'Just for two weeks.'

'—just for two weeks, and we collect these wonderful things from the beach. Skate egg-cases, cuttlefish bones—'

'—fancy pebbles. We find they're full of the mystery of the sea, but without the *fear*, if you know what I mean.'

10

Topsails furled, helm lashed, guns secured, running before the Cape Horn gale, thought the parrot, half the crew in irons and the rest blind drunk, only the captain awake, accompanying his trusty parrot on the concertina and praying to the Devil for a bluewater run to a safe haven in the Dry Tortegas and a big mulatto whore, that was what the sea was all about.

'—and we've got it all set up next to this rather nice *fin-de-siècle* sofa in lavender Dralon we had done. We call it Yellow Book corner, don't we, Adrian?'

'I think I've probably got just the thing you're looking for,' said the owner, 'if you'd care to pop downstairs.'

He showed them through a green baize door, and followed, leaving the parrot alone once more, inescapably tethered in the window among the genteel bric-à-brac. Small boys passed, flashing V-signs and banging pocket computer-games on the glass, two entwined drunks staggered across the road from the pub opposite and screamed POLLY WANTS A CRACKER! at him twenty times over until they managed to roll howling away like a hysterical octopus, a very old metermaid came and stared at him for ten minutes without doing anything except forage aimlessly in her starboard nostril with a felt-tipped pen.

A mange-pocked semi-airedale, free as the wind and ostensibly ownerless, barked at him derisively and then underwrote its scorn by lifting its leg, slowly and deliberately, against the bollard, cunningly fashioned from a Peninsular cannon, which the owner had cemented beside the shop's step as a commercial *leitmotif*.

Iron entered the parrot's soul. To have Israel Hands beside him, blasting his enemies left and right from a brace of looted Spanish horse-pistols! To see the metermaid spitted on Silver's cutlass like a stuck pig! To lie a mile off Banbury High Street, broadside on, strike the Jolly Roger, and let three tiers of gundeck wipe the ledger clean!

The green baize door opened again, and the two customers minced excitedly back into the shop, clutching a lamp between them and blowing him a farewell kiss. The owner followed, with a bowl which he set beside the parrot on the column. The parrot stared at it. Little protein-enriched soya cinders stared back at him. He wondered what paw-paw tasted like, or yams, or breadfruit; an atavistic yearning to peel a kumquat made

11

his very beak hurt.

Little else happened as the afternoon bleakened into night. A large woman came in to negotiate for a Queen Anne breakfront bookcase, but not until the parrot had been removed on the grounds of smell and psittacine infection. A dealer turned up with six Adam fireplaces wrested from a demolished manse and offered the parrot a large walnut, which turned out to be made of plaster and to have broken off a baroque flourish on one of the mantels, this discovery not, however, being made until the parrot had driven itself half-mad and the dealer had laughed himself half-sick. And ten minutes before closing-time, a passer-by dropped in to make a bid for the parrot itself, since his decor required a nice stuffed parrot to set off a wallful of stag-heads in his newly refurbished den; upon being informed that this was a live parrot, the man replied that that was no problem, anyone could stuff a bloody parrot, he had a book at home. He was, he said, prepared to go as high as a ton.

The owner said he would think about it.

After which he pulled down the blind, locked up, and went home.

The hours passed, variously signalled by a number of long-cased clocks which, despite their long familiarity, never failed to knock the parrot off his perch, shattering his poignant dreams of plunder and lagoon; and thus it was that, at 3.02 am, when the jemmy forced the green baize door from the basement, the parrot was already awake and alert. Independently, his two eyes swivelled towards the sound, straining through the gloom, until a torch snapped on and, in its shielded glow, he saw two neckless, barrel-chested men, in stocking masks and rubber gloves, carrying—his heart leapt, banging—plastic bags and sawn-off shotguns!

For some time he watched them scout the shelves, picking and peering, assessing this Derby shepherdess, that Chelsea vase, squinting at hallmarks, feeling veneers; then he cried:

'*What about the real stuff! What about the real stuff!*'

They sprang erect, the guns came up, the hammers clicked back; a Minton urn, one of a pair, fell and shattered.

'Don't shoot, Fred's a clever boy!' shrieked the parrot. 'Who knows where the safe is? Who knows where the safe is?'

At last the stockinged heads, like giant saveloys, located him.

'Glimey!' muttered one, liplessly. 'It's a gloody carrot, Charlie!'

Cautiously, they crept towards him, until he could see their tattooed forearms, smell the gun-oil, taste their very villainy.

'The safe's behind the walnut tallboy!' he cackled. 'The safe's behind the walnut tallboy!'

They did not hesitate long. Expertly, soundlessly, they eased the tallboy from the wall. The safe-door stood revealed.

'Gloody congination lock!' said one.

The other stripped off his stocking, and approached the parrot.

'Any ideas?' he said.

The parrot glowed, inside. Had he tears, he would have shed them, now.

'7834 left, 9266 right!' he cried. '7834 left, 9266 right!'

And so it proved. The door swung wide. Slowly, carefully—for the real stuff was very real indeed—the plastic bags were filled, and the safe was emptied. And when it was done, the two men came up to the parrot, and patted his beak. And one put his eye close to the parrot's—and a terrible eye it was, thought the parrot deliriously, it could have been Captain Morgan's eye, it could have been *Silver's* eye—and said:

'Thanks, mate!'

But as they turned to steal away, the other paused, and turned.

'Here,' he murmured, 'you wouldn't tell no-one he called me Charlie, would you? You wouldn't give no-one a description or nothing?'

The parrot cackled quietly to itself, for a second or two, in its private joy. It put its head on one side.

'No chance!' it said. 'No chance!'

No Bloody Fear

HOTEL FOR PHOBICS

Britain's first hotel for phobics has opened in Firbeck Avenue, Skegness, helped by £42,000 from the Government's small firm guarantee loan. Mr Tony Elliott, founder of Nottinghamshire Phobics Association, said: "People may have all sorts of psychological problems and we will try to look after them at the seaside."

Daily Telegraph

DEAR SYLVIA,

Well here we all are, safe and sound if you do not count Norman's hairpiece blowing off coming from the station, that is one of the little penalties of having to keep your head stuck out of cab windows, I am always on at him to get his claustrophobia looked at but it is not easy to find a doctor who will see him in the middle of a field. We would have stopped to retrieve it, but a gull was on it like a bloody bullet, it is probably halfway up a cliff by now with three eggs in it.

Sorry, Sylve, I had to break off there for a minute, it was writing *cliff* did it, one of my little turns come on, I had to put my head between my knees and suck an Extra Strong, I do not have to tell *you* why, I know; remember that time before we was married and you and me went to the Locarno, Streatham, and that ginger bloke sitting by the spot-prize display asked me to dance, and when he got on his feet he was about six feet nine and I brought my Guinness up?

Anyway, we got to the hotel all right, apart from Norman's bloody mother trying to avoid stepping on the pavement cracks between the cab and the gate and walking into a gravel bin, she come down a hell of a wallop and her case burst open and her collection of bottle tops was bouncing all over the place, it took us near on two hours to get her into her room in the cellar on account of no lift below ground floor, so the management had to bag her up and winch her down through the coal chute, all on account of she can't get to sleep unless she hears rats running about. Still, one consolation is that that's the last we'll see of the old bat for two weeks, due to where

Norman will not go inside, Tracy comes out in blackheads if there's no windows, big Kevin is allergic to hot water pipes, little Barry gets diarrhoea in the presence of rodents, and me, well, you know about me and bottle tops!

The landlady was ever so nice about Norman. They had a bed all made up for him in the shrubbery, no plants so big he couldn't see over them if he began to panic in the night, and a very nice man near him, but not *too* near, who sleeps in the middle of the lawn with his foot roped to a sundial in the event of gravity suddenly stopping and him falling off into space. Turned out they had a lot of army experience in common: they both had boots as pets, during National Service.

My room is quite nice, too, lots of things to arrange: you can stand the coffee table on the tallboy and put the hearthrug on it with the potty on top, and if you turn the potty upside down you'll find it's large enough to stand a hairspray aerosol on it. Of course, it's all getting a bit high by then, but it looks lower if you stand on the bed, so I'm quite happy really, even if I can't have Tracy sharing with me due to bees figuring prominently in the wallpaper, and I can't visit her, either, on account of they've put her on the top floor. It's all expense, Sylve, isn't it? Still, we managed to get big Kevin and little Barry to share: the management found them a triangular room, so they've got a corner each to stand in, leaving only one for them to keep an eye on; they can get quite a lot of sleep, in turns.

Mealtimes are great fun, everybody is ever so sociable, there's a very nice man from Norwich I think it is, who comes round to every table just after we've all sat down and touches every single piece of cutlery, and two charming sisters from Doncaster who eat standing on their chairs due to the possibility of mice turning up sudden, and a former postmaster who sings 'Nola' whenever there's oxtail soup. My Norman has been a great hit, due to not coming in for meals: everybody takes it in turns to go to the window and feed him, also give him little titbits to carry over to his friend tied to the sundial, because the waitress has agoraphobia and can't even look at the forecourt without going green.

Not that there aren't little squabbles from time to time: Sunday, we had plums and custard, and little Barry likes to arrange the stones on the side of his dish. What he did not

15

realize was that this makes Mr Noles from Gants Hill, who is on our table, punch people in the mouth. Big Kevin, as you know, is not called big Kevin for nothing and has had to learn to look after himself from an early age, due to where his father is unable to come inside and help him, big Kevin took hold of Mr Noles by his collar and chucked him out into the corridor, which was a terrible thing to do, it turned out, because Mr Noles has a horrible fear of narrow places and pays £2 per day extra to enter the dining-room via the fire-escape, but big Kevin was not to know this, he is only a boy, though getting enormous enough for me to feel queasy every time I stretch up to make sure he's brushed his teeth. The upshot of it was, Mr Noles was hurling himself about in the corridor for close on twenty minutes before Mrs Noles could get a net over him. He broke eighteen plaster ducks, three barometers, and put his elbow straight through 'The Monarch of the Glen', though doing less damage than you might think since its face had already been painted out on account of the night porter having a morbid fear of antlers.

And all the time my Norman is shouting *'What's going on? What's bloody going on?'* from the garden, deeply distressing his friend tied to the sundial who can hear all this breakage and shrieking and reckons gravity is beginning to pack up and bring things off the walls.

Still, it turned out all right, Mr Noles and big Kevin made it up, they have a lot in common, basically, both being unable to walk down a street without picking bits off hedges, and he asked big Kevin to join him on the beach because Mrs Noles never went there on account of her terror of being buried alive. She likes to spend her afternoons standing on the concrete forecourt with a big bell in her hand and a whistle between her teeth in case of emergencies, so her husband and big Kevin and little Barry and Tracy and Norman and me all went off to the beach. Trouble was, it would all have been all right if Norman's new friend hadn't been unsettled by the false alarm over gravity: he did not want to be left alone, so the porter found a huge coil of rope so that Norman's new friend could come down to the beach without untying himself from the sundial, but it was nearly three hundred yards and you have to go round two corners, so you can't see what's going on behind, and what happened was the rope got caught in a car bumper and one moment Norman's new friend was cautiously creeping along beside us, and the next he was suddenly plucked from our midst.

We visited him in the cottage hospital, but even our presence (minus, of course, Norman, also Tracy, who faints in the vicinity of linoleum) could not persuade him that he had not fallen off Earth and hurt himself dropping onto some alien planet. His argument was that we had fallen with him but, being unencumbered by rope or sundials, had managed to land on our feet, unhurt, and were keeping the truth from him so as not to alarm an injured man.

There was no convincing him, so we just left him there and collected Norman and Tracy and went down to the beach to find big Kevin and Mr Noles. But all we could find was big Kevin, he was huddled under a stack of deck-chairs and sobbing: we ran up to him (all except little Barry, who was terrified in case the shadow of the deck-chairs fell on his foot), and asked him what was wrong, and he said he had been getting on fine, he had buried Mr Noles in the sand, because Mr Noles had been told by his psychiatrist that this was a very good way to overcome his fear of narrow spaces, and he was just about to stick a little windmill over where he had buried him when a crab come out of the sea and started running towards him sideways.

We all gasped!

'It is my own fault,' shouted Norman, from a nice open space he had found in between the airbeds, 'I knew the lad was an arachnophobe, it never occurred to me that he would associate crabs with spiders, that is not the sort of thing what occurs to a claustrophobe on account of you never get near enough to anything to distinguish it.'

'So what happened, big Kevin?' I said, aghast.

'I run off, Mum,' he sobbed. 'I must have run miles.'

A cold chill shot down my spine, as if I'd just seen the Eiffel Tower or something.

'Where is Mr Noles buried?' I enquired, gently.

I think you probably know the answer to that, Sylve. I tell you, we prodded lolly-sticks all over that beach for five hours, i.e. well after it was too late anyway, and no luck. It was getting dark before I knew I would have to be the one to break the news to Mrs Noles. Her of all people.

She was still standing on the forecourt when we got back to the hotel. I put my hand on her arm.

'How are you, Mrs Noles?' I murmured.

'Nicely, thank you,' she replied. 'I got a bit worried around half-past four. The sun was very hot, and I thought: any minute, this asphalt is going to melt and swallow me up. But it didn't.'

Quick is best, I said to myself, Sylve. So I come right out and told her that Mr Noles had been buried alive. And do you know what she said?

'Serves him right, the stingy bastard,' she said. 'I always told him we ought to have bought a bell each.'

That's the best thing about holidays, Sylve, I always say: you meet so many interesting people.

It takes you right out of yourself.

Your loving friend, Sharon.

Just a Snog at Twilight

The night Head Proof Reader at the Guardian retired last night.—
Guardian

HE STROLLED to the window, and gazed out over the darkling
garden. It was strange, not to be girding his loins for the office,
not to be sharpening his pencils, not to be buffing his eyeshield,
not to be drawing on the snug regulation armbands to hold
back his spotless cuffs against the omnipresent threat of
undried ink.

He sighed; and murmured:

'The curlew tolls the knee of farting day,
The lowing herd wing slowly o'er the leg,
The pluoghman homeark Rangers 3,
Luton 788 (after extra tile).'

He sighed again, and turned from the window, and glanced
at his fine presentation bracket clock bearing the brass-plated
legend GOOD DUCK FROM ALL YOUR OLD FRIENDS
AT THE NAURGIAD, and even as the tear pricked his eye, a
blush suffused his cheek: he was no prude, but seeing the word
DUCK in print like that, no asterisks, did, he had to admit, go
against the grain. Ah, well, times changed; this was, after all,
9128.

The clock struck forty-three, and he reached for his coat.

'Shrdlg!' he called. 'WzWzWzWzWzWz.'

'All right,' his wife called back from the kitchen, 'but don't
be long.'

They had been married for many years.

How odd it was, being out in the evening, in his local, yet unfamiliar, streets: all his working life, he had never been out much. Nights were spent at the *Guardian*, days were spent either sleeping or struggling with the crossword. He had started it in 1937, and it had become a totally absorbing hobby: once, early in 1953, he had nearly got a clue, but it eluded him at the last hurdle. He felt in his bones what the answer to 'Did it carry Hannibal's trunk?' must surely be, but *enelurg* did not have the specified eight letters. The crossword was yellow, now, and brittle, after forty-five years of devoted fingering, but he was a persistent man, and he would not give up easily. Perhaps now, with the elbow-room of retirement . . .

But it had inevitably meant that his local experience had been severely restricted, and it was not without a certain frisson of excitement that he entered the tobacconist's, thus breaking the purchasing habits of a long lifetime spent in the kiosks of EC4, where the familiar traders well knew his little ways.

'Good evening,' he said, 'may I have a packet of pork-tipped Serion Verses and a box of cont. foot of page 4, column 6?'

The girl twitched the sari more snugly about her slim shoulder, and looked uncertainly at him.

'I am begging your pardon?' she said. 'What are these items that you are requesting?'

He rolled his eyes, and shook his head. Years of meticulous attention to the *Guardian*'s resolutely egalitarian pages had, of course, left him free of all prejudice, but it had to be said that righteous impatience tended to take hold of him when he was confronted with those whose English did not quite conform to the flawless standards set in Farringdon Road.

'Good heavens, madam!' he cried. 'You act as if you had never heard of them!'

At the cry, the proprietor himself emerged from the back of the shop.

'What is appearing to be the trouble?' he enquired.

'This gentleman,' replied the assistant, 'is asking for some, er—'

'Serion Verses,' snapped the ex-Head Proof Reader. 'A perfectly ordinary packet of figs.'

The proprietor beamed broadly, and slipped the brass

knuckles back into his apron-pocket, discreetly.

'Aha!' he exclaimed. 'That is immediately explaining it! We are not selling figs, sir. That is not being our business.'

'Dog Almighty!' cried the customer. 'I can see the bloody things on the shelf behind take in additional copy Minister said toady upon retuning to $1\frac{7}{8}$ Downing Streen where delete Sputh China Sea insert Her Majesty the Queer!'

The proprietor slid his hand into his apron-pocket again.

'If you are not leaving my premises immediately,' he muttered, pushing his weeping assistant for her own safety behind a sturdy display of slightly shop-soiled and greatly reduced walnut whips, 'I am having no other course which is being open to me but to call the policemen. Good evening.'

The customer ground his teeth, and clenched his fists, but turned, finally, upon his heel, and stamped out of the shop.

'Send 'em all back to Panistak!' he cried; but not until he was well out of earshot, and not without an uneasy pang at this shattering breach in what had hitherto been a lifetime's unwavering commitment. Indeed, so disturbed was he by the incident that he did not see the group of youths until he backed heavily into them.

'OY!' shouted the leader. 'Are you asking to have your bleeding face trod on, grandpa?'

'Are you asking to carry your teeth home in your bleeding hat?' enquired a second.

'Would you care to end up,' said a third, removing a cycle-chain from his boot, 'as two gross of Big Macs?'

The ex-Head Proof Reader raised placating hands.

'Lads!' he declared. 'We at the *Naurgiad* have always been on your side! We understand your problems. The Hole Secretary is a crenit, it is the enviro6 which is set this italic bold condensed, it is the lack of yobs which is the cause.'

'What?' said the leader, through gritted teeth.

'Yobs!' shouted the perspiring well-wisher. 'That is what is at the bottom of street violets! Britain's yob-centres are—'

'He ain't 'alf asking for it,' grunted the second youth. 'Shall we do him?'

The leader put his face close to his victim.

'Eff off!' he snarled.

'I beg your pardon?'

'Spell it out for him, Brian.'

So Brian spelt it out. The ex-Head Proof Reader smiled, and tutted, and shook his head.

'No, no, no,' he murmured. 'Forgive me, but it would have to be *Dee off*. Not, of course, that one blames you, the shocking state of our education syrglb is—'

After they blacked his eye and he was sitting on the pavement, they aerosoled the word upon his mackintosh, so that he would no longer be in doubt, and strolled whistling away.

It was thus not entirely unsurprising that when he eventually struggled to his feet and staggered in the hope of assistance towards two women, one of whom was wheeling a push-chair, they took one look at his wild expression, his torn collar, his disarranged clothing, and, above all perhaps, the bizarre message painted on his coat, and immediately screamed: 'RAPE!'

He reeled, horror-stricken.

'No!' he shrieked. '*Me*? Have you any idea to whom you are in yesterday's editions we refurned to Ms Manny Whitehouse as Ms Manny Whitehouse, this should of course have read Ms Manny Whitehouse, we have always been—'

'RAPE!'

'—the leading spokespersons in the defence of ladypersons against the oppression of gentlemanpersons! Great Dog in Hendon, ladypersons, we have stood up for buttered wives, yob equality, gay liberace, onanparent families, 7689.34% on demand, free contraceptive pails, we have Errol Pizza, Jim the Tweeney, Pony Siddons . . .'

'I'm afraid we had to put him in this jacket, madam,' said the first policeman.

She stared at the wretched face gazing out of the swaddling canvas at her.

'Didn't he try to explain?' she enquired.

'It was after he tried to explain,' said the second policeman, 'that we put him in the canvas jacket.'

The police surgeon came into the charge room, wiping his hands on a paper towel. He smiled.

'Well,' he said, 'he was definitely not drunk. Personally, I don't think there's anything you can charge him with.'

'What's his trouble, then?' asked the first policeman.

The police surgeon crumpled the paper towel, and tossed it into the metal waste-bin.

'I'd say,' he replied, weighing his words professionally, 'that he was suffering from an inability to distinguish between the *Guardian* and real life.'

'There's a lot of it about,' said the second policeman.

The ex-Head Proof Reader's red-rimmed eyes swivelled towards the police surgeon's face. He licked dry lips.

'Is there a worm for it?' he said.

O Little Town of Cricklewood

I DO not expect you to remember it, but I have mentioned our new neighbours before. It is one of the small perks of being a hack that one can very occasionally vent publicly things that cannot otherwise be de-chested. I am not proud of it, but sometimes it is the only alternative to roping the throat to an RSJ and kicking away the bentwood chair. I hope you'll understand.

Not that the imminent occasion is anywhere near as dire as the last, when the thirteen children of, let us call him Chief Paramount, all came home from Stowe and Roedean for the summer hols and, slipping out of their First XI blazers and navy knickers and into initially rather fetching ethnic clobber, threw a party which went on next door for six days and nights and employed a good eighty per cent of all the steel bands east of Tobago. No shortage of instruments for late-arriving guests to have an amateur bang on, either, doubtless because Chief Paramount owns a sizeable whack of the Nigerian oil industry, and the drums just keep on coming.

He also enjoys diplomatic status. Indeed, it would be hard to find anyone who enjoyed it more. The family hobby is parking on zebra crossings, sideways, and building peculiar baroque extensions to their house which would not only require planning permission but also a Special Royal Commission on Suburban Blight if they were perpetrated by anyone not in a position to torpedo the next Commonwealth Games if he's not allowed to build a lighthouse where his coalshed used to be.

Thus, we do not complain. It would be un-neighbourly as well as futureless to do so formally, and it is difficult to do so informally because not only is Chief Paramount in Nigeria all the time, but there are three Mrs Paramounts. I learned this when I called to enquire which of their thirteen heirs had flattened the party-fence, and had a long and interesting conversation with what I had taken to be the lad's mother, only to discover that I had picked the wrong mother. I assume the Chief to be a Muslim, or perhaps just careless.

Anyway, this multispousal situation lies at the root of my present little difficulty. We have occasionally dropped a note in next door, inviting the Chief to a gin and Twiglet, but he has always been abroad; he will, however, be home for Christmas, we learned from his manciple (now living in a tasty Gothic folly which appeared at the end of the garden only quite recently), and since we throw an annual Boxing Day party for our neighbours, we have decided to invite him in.

Them in.

You see the problem immediately, I know. It occurred to *me*, of course, only after, milliseconds after, their letterbox-flap had snapped over my note: *I do not know how to entertain a man with three wives.*

They will come in. The room will be jovial, hot, mistletoe-hung, and full of guests mulled into a sense of false bonhomie. Do I say: 'May I introduce Chief and Mrs Paramount and Mrs Paramount and Mrs Paramount? Or simply 'This is Chief and the Mrs Paramounts'? In that case, other guests would naturally start attempting to establish which was his wife, which his mother, which his sister-in-law, to be followed by all kinds of embarrassments about who looked too young to be what, and so forth. Should I, therefore, take a positive, no-nonsense approach: 'This is Chief Paramount and his wife. The lovely lady in the long puce number is his other wife, ha-ha-ha, and that's his third wife over by the bookcase, in the green silk suit.'

I know these silences that open up at parties. Some prat is bound to step into the vacuum and start wittering on about how civilised it is to get on socially with one's ex, oh you all *live* together next door, do you, how extremely sophisticated, you people can still teach us primitive honkies a thing or two, ha-ha-ha, would you care for a prawn cracker, tell me, is it true, don't be offended, that . . .

Worse (probably), is there a pecking order in a three-wife situation? Does the tall one in the puce, having brought the largest number of heifers to the marriage, get to be introduced first? Or is that the prerogative of the green silk suit, who happens to be the seventh daughter of the seventh son of a Witch Consultant? Maybe the one next to him is Top Wife, having borne him the first of the thirteen, who can tell?

Tread on the wrong corn, and they'll all be off next door again in unscalable dudgeon, on the blower to Geoffrey Howe and making plans to build an unpermitted heliport on the roof of the unpermitted Gothic butlerdome.

Which brings me to the Saudis on the corner. Moved in last August when the hitherto resident shirt manufacturer retired to Marbella, but not a lot of social contact since, couple of curt nods in September, a brief smile in October, I think it was, when a cat got run over and everybody came out to wonder which of us ought to peel it off the road (guess who drew the short straw), but that was only with *him*. Nothing from his wife, if that's what he keeps inside the black sheet I occasionally spot nipping in and out of his Mercedes. Just a pair of eyes over the veil, could be anybody in there, they might be gay for all I know.

Anyway, we've asked them in for Boxing Day, too.

How are they going to get on with the Paramounts? I suppose they're all Muslim, so there's an ice-breaker, but is that going to be enough, I ask myself? 'Welcome, Mr and is it Mrs Ibn Ben Cornerhouse, I don't think you know the four Paramounts, did you realize you're all Muslims, there's a turn-up for the book, ha-ha-ha, what a small world, do you have sprouts with the turkey in your country to commemorate the birth of the Prophet, I've always wondered, haven't I, darling, I don't think you know Mrs Coren, by the way. No, Chief, just the one, ha-ha-ha . . .'

The thing is, there are clearly different varieties of Mohammedan. Especially when it comes to wives. The Mrs Paramounts are all voluptuous, cheery, extrovert, whereas Mrs Ibn Ben Cornerhouse goes out in a shroud and avoids any eye-contact. There may even be half a dozen of *her* across the road, no way of telling, one length of black lagging is much like another, what do I do if six Mrs Ibn Ben Cornerhouses turn up and refuse to be distinguished, let alone introduced?

I bet none of them eats prawn dip, either. We shall have to watch the dietary strictures, or there could well be bloodshed.

26

You know Arabs, very short fuses, plus great store set by social protocols and host-incumbency, my house is your house, all that: we shall probably have to get in sheep's eyes or something to pass round, and how can you tell if they're any good or not, I'm not tasting them, that's for sure, we shall just have to rely on the good name of Sainsburys, they couldn't afford to put duff optics on their shelves, keeping the Arabs sweet is the only edge they've got over Marks and Sparks.

It's just occurred to me that Muslims don't drink. I think. There can be no other excuse for mint tea. I bet the Paramounts knock it back, mind, I still remember that week-long summer party, they had people laid out three-deep on their gravel drive, you don't get that way on Tizer, it's definitely a different branch, I was right. I hope to God they're not incompatible, I seem to recall something about Sunnis and Shi-ites, that's all I need on Boxing Day, big Muslim punch-up in the front room and the Ibn Ben Cornerhouses sprinting home to start lobbing mortars on the house next door.

I've just remembered dancing. Not that we plan it, it is simply that there is a gramophone, all right musicentre, we like to have a bit of background Albinoni to start off with, but after the first few bottles of Old Sporran have gone about their eviscerating business, someone or other of the regulars fishes out some warped Dixieland relic of my *jeunesse d'Ory*, lurches the pick-up arm onto it, and grabs someone else's better, or occasionally worse, half in that desperate Yuletide bid for a seasonally-endorsed grope, until, before very long, those unpartnered may stand quietly by the window, tactfully ignoring the Saturnalia at their backs, and watch the tiles coming off the roof.

I do not know how this will go down with Mrs Ibn Ben Cornerhouse.

Yes I do.

God knows how they order these things at the Foreign and Commonwealth Office. They probably have a book. In The Event Of A Dusky Husband Turning Up Mob-handed, The First Wife Receives A Cheese Football From The Host's Elder Unmarried Son, The Second Wife Has The First Dance With The Hostess's Youngest Brother From Lowestoft (Except During Ramadan), The Third Wife Is Shown The Host's

Collection Of Great British Beermats, The Fourth . . . They must be up to their eyes in small etiquettular print, no wonder they didn't notice Galtieri's lads trundling their boats out. Put an inadvertent hand on a shapely bum at the annual FO tea-dance and you could be looking down the wrong end of an oil embargo in less time than it takes to tell.

Thinking of which, it occurs to me that I do not know Ibn Ben Cornerhouse's line of country, but it must, surely, be oil, too, in which case he and Paramount could well be at extremely nasty loggerheads. How do Saudi Arabia and Nigeria get on? Did they meet in the qualifying round of the World Cup, and if so, who won? Do they even recognize one another? Am I letting myself in for some fearful United Nations scene, all the wives snapping their reticules shut on a single prearranged signal, chucking their crisps in the air, and storming out *en masse* to draft Stern Notes to the premises across the road?

Words cannot adequately encompass (I have tried Roget, but he obviously lived in a different street) the bleak apprehension with which I face the season of goodwill currently rumbling towards me. I don't even have room left, fortunately, to tell you about the gown manufacturers, on the other side of us from the Paramounts, who think that Menachem Begin is an appeaser. They haven't met the Ibn Ben Cornerhouses yet.

They will on the 26th, though. I suppose there is nothing for it but to keep the fingers crossed and hope against hope for the best.

It is, after all, Christmas.

Moscow or Bust

A claim was made last week that Napoleon died of a hormone-abnormality disease that was slowly turning him into a woman. This, according to The Journal of Sexual Medicine, *explains contemporary reports of Napoleon's highly feminine appearance.*

One of his doctors described the general's body as 'effeminate', another said he had 'a chest that many a woman would be proud of', while one wrote that 'the emperor has small white hands and shows a good leg'. Even Josephine compared her lover to a castrato. —Observer

AS SOON as the first pale ray of watery spring sun slid through his curtains and struck his beard, Mr Sam Kaminski sighed, eased his elderly body from the bed, shuffled resignedly downstairs, and began to board up his shop window.

For spring, though naturally enough greeted with ecstasy by most of Mother Russia, brought nothing but anxiety to the ghetto of Plotz: as winter thawed, Plotz, on the barren banks of the River Niemen, gritted its teeth, prayed its prayers, and waited for the worst.

At the noise of Kaminski's hammer, his neighbour, still in his nightshirt, rushed out into the unpaved street.

'Did they come yet?' he cried.

Kaminski shook his head.

'Precautions,' he said, through a mouthful of nails.

His neighbour stared at his own window. It was full of blouses.

'Could lose my entire stock,' he muttered. 'It's been a bad winter.'

Kaminski spat out his last nail and banged it home.

'It makes a difference?' he said.

'With blouses,' replied his neighbour, 'it makes a *big* difference.'

'How come?'

'The whores don't go home,' replied his neighbour. 'That's how come. They stay in the barracks maybe six months. The normal rate is a blouse a month. Figure for yourself.'

'With furs,' said Kaminski, 'it's different. I got a class trade. Officers only. For their wives.'

'Could be a nice little business,' said his neighbour. 'If they paid.'

'If they paid,' said Kaminski, 'it could be a terrific business. I could be a chain by now. Mail order, even.'

'Don't joke,' said his neighbour.

Kaminski sighed, and went back into his shop, and took the best coats down to the cellar. Then he came back, slowly, up the steps, put on his black homburg with the reinforced steel lining, and waited for the Cossacks.

It was nearly noon before the first hoofbeats shook the shuttered town. Kaminski cocked a practised ear, assessing his personal time-table: they would stop at the butcher's for a little rape, the way they did every spring, then they would burn down the school, say fifteen minutes, after that they would probably—he tensed, gasped! His heart lurched, missed, lurched irregularly on: they were *not* stopping! The thunder of hooves grew louder, shaking the wooden walls, then suddenly died in a jangle of tack and a rasp of dismounting boots, outside his very door!

Fists banged upon it.

'We're out of stock!' cried the furrier. 'We're awaiting deliveries! Could be a month, but I can't promise, maybe a—'

The door flew from its hinges.

'All right!' shouted Kaminski, leaping up. 'Okay! I lied, I admit it, I got a nice musquash stole, mink it isn't, but in a good light—'. He stopped.

The figure in the doorway was very small, for a Cossack. The uniform was unfamiliar. The hat was most peculiar. And the perfume, in particular, was very expensive. Most Cossacks wore wolfdung.

Kaminski took an uncertain step towards the doorway.

'Yes?' he said.

The short figure drilled Kaminski with two glittering eyes.

'I am Napoleon,' it announced, 'Emperor of Europe!'

Kaminski reeled, and clutched for support at the cutting-table.

'So!' he cried. 'You have invaded at last! You are looking for Moscow! Okay, so you turn left at the—'

'Yes,' said Napoleon, holding up a beautiful little hand, 'and no. Yes, I have invaded, and no, I am not looking for Moscow. What I am looking for is something in sable, full-length, with a raglan sleeve. Chic, but not ostentatious.'

As Kaminski gaped, and mopped his face, a tall and iron-jawed man strode into the little shop, and bowed stiffly.

'May I urge Your Imperial Highness to make haste?' he said.

'No,' said Napoleon. 'You don't rush sable, Ney. Am I right, Mr, er—'

'Kaminski,' said the furrier. 'Absolutely, Your Imperial Highness! I can see Your Imperial Highness is an Imperial Highness of terrific taste. With sable, artistry is what you have to have, also skill, also the experience of a lifetime, never mind a—by the way, Your Imperial Highness, what is this raglan sleeve business? We at Kaminski Bespoke Furs like to think of ourselves as being in the forefront of—'

Napoleon smiled, not without smugness. His kiss-curl bobbed.

'It could be a whole new fashion,' he said.

'French, naturally,' said Kaminski, nodding, 'such taste, your people, such what shall I say, such—'

'As a matter of fact,' said Napoleon, 'no. You may recall the storming of Badajoz during the Peninsular War?'

'I read about it in the *Fur Trade Gazette*,' nodded Kaminski. 'A terrible business. Persian lamb prices shot right down.'

Napoleon glared at him.

'At Badajoz,' he said, his voice rising to a not unfetching soprano, 'there was this absolutely *ravishing* English officer, wasn't there, Ney?'

The marshal looked out of the doorway, and sucked his gilt chinstrap.

'Anyway,' continued Napoleon, 'he was wearing this wonderful frogged jacket, sort of half off-the-shoulder, with a very full—'

'You could sketch it, maybe?' suggested Kaminski.

'Your Imperial Highness,' said Ney, as Bonaparte licked his crayon, rolling his eyes and tutting creatively by turns, 'we have 435,000 men of the Grande Armée awaiting Your Imperial Highness's orders to advance, and while we have the brief meteorological advantage afforded us in this God-forsaken spot, we—'

'Leave us, Ney!' snapped Napoleon. After his marshal had stamped furiously out, he drew Kaminski confidentially into a dark corner of the shop.

'You don't think I'm a little, er, short for a full-length coat? I should hate to look squat.'

'Take off the topcoat,' said Kaminski. He took the coat, hung it up, turned, closed one eye, considering. 'Your Imperial Highness has a terrific figure,' he said finally.

'But not a little, er, *full*,' giggled Napoleon, 'here?'

Kaminski tutted professionally.

'Since when was a big bust a disadvantage? Be grateful. It gives you presence. Also, you have nice slim legs. What we call a pocket Venus in the fur trade, you should pardon my familiarity. In sable you'll be a knockout, believe me. Would I lie?'

Napoleon smiled, and squeezed Kaminski's arm.

'Measure me,' he breathed.

The Grande Armée bivouacked on the banks of the Niemen, confused, disgruntled, while their Emperor waited for his first fitting. Ney began to drink heavily. Most nights, Napoleon waited up for him, and the camp rang to his subsequent screaming complaints. During the day, they argued about the coat.

A week later, Napoleon returned to Kaminski Bespoke Furs.

'It fits you,' said the furrier, 'like the paper on the wall! You and that coat were made for each other.'

Napoleon minced back and forth in front of the triple-mirror.

'It makes me look hippy,' he said at last.

'Let me take it in a bit at the back,' offered Kaminski.

On the banks of the Niemen, two divisions of Prussian infantry deserted.

By early August (having been sent back twice, to have white ermine cuffs added, and to have a matching hat made up), the coat was ready. Kaminski sent a messenger out to the camp, who returned with Napoleon, and a hollow-eyed muttering Ney.

'Elegant,' said Napoleon. 'I'll take it.'

'Thank God!' croaked Marshal Ney. 'Can we go to Moscow now?'

'Shall I wrap it?' asked Kaminski. 'I'll find a smart box.'

'I'll wear it,' said Napoleon. 'If you've got it, flaunt it!'

Kaminski's neighbour came out, along with the rest of Plotz, to watch the Grande Armée pull out.

'Did he pay, at least?' enquired the neighbour.

Kaminski showed him the cheque.

'Cash it quick,' said the neighbour. 'I understand the Tsar managed to get a big army together.'

Three weeks later, in the middle of the night, a stone crashed through Kaminski's window. He sprang up, poised for Cossacks, and glanced outside.

'My spurs keep catching in the lining,' shouted Napoleon, from the head of his army, who stretched, bleary-eyed, from Kaminski Bespoke Furs to the moonlit horizon.

'I'll come down,' said Kaminski.

He lit a few candles, and examined the coat.

'I didn't notice at first,' said Napoleon. 'I got involved in my new hair-style. I couldn't think of anything else. You know how it happens.'

'One ringlet is very fashionable,' said Kaminski. 'Where did you get the gloves?'

'Szolov,' replied the Emperor. 'They made me up eighty pairs.'

'It took two weeks,' said Ney.

'I'll have to shorten the coat a little,' said Kaminski.

'Moscow,' said Ney, and fell on his bottle.

Two days later, with autumn chill already in the September air, Napoleon strutted up and down outside Kaminski's, testing the new length. Kaminski and his neighbour watched him, respectfully, from the shop.

'A pity he keeps the hand inside the coat all the time,' murmured Kaminski. 'It's ruining the shape.'

'He's a Frenchman,' said his neighbour, grinning. 'Maybe he likes to keep his hand on his winkle.'

'What winkle?' said Kaminski.

The Emperor came back inside the shop.

'Perfect,' he said, and was about to leave when his eye rested on Kaminski's rack. '*What's that?*' he shrilled.

'Chinchilla,' replied Kaminski. 'The best.'

'I'll take it!' shrieked Napoleon.

'It's not Your Imperial Highness's size,' said Kaminski.

Napoleon waved his hand impatiently.

'Then make me one up!'

'With chinchilla,' said Kaminski, 'it could take three weeks minimum.'

'I'll wait,' said Napoleon firmly.

'But Moscow!' cried Kaminski. 'Not that I couldn't do with the business, but didn't you already waste enough time?'

Napoleon stamped his pretty foot furiously.

'Moscow, Moscow, Moscow!' he screamed. 'Why is everybody in such a *rush* to get to Moscow?'

And even as he spoke, in the little street beyond the shop, the first pale snowflake floated down and settled on Ney's sleeve.

Sixty Vainglorious Years

DURING the highpoint week of BBC Radio's thrilling Golden Jubilee celebrations, I could not help wandering into the BBC Club in Langham Place in the hope of fetching up against Wynford Danvers Nerd MBE, known to everyone at Broadcasting House as the doyen's doyen, to see if he would be prepared to reminisce a little about his part in the great days of radio. I was indeed in luck: despite the fact that he had just recorded his eightieth broadcast of the week entitled *We Called It Wireless* and was awaiting the fireman's lift which would take him to his eighty-first, his eyes nevertheless lit up through the bottom of his glass at the chance for just one more stroll down memory lane . . .

COREN Tell me, is it true that you . . .
NERD Ha, ha, ha! Yes, I had a feeling you'd bring that one up, after sixty years in this game one gets a sort of a, call it a sixth sense about what's coming next, unlike some modern broadcasters I could, well, no names, no pack drill, as we used to say at Savoy Hill, you were, of course, going to ask me about being the first man ashore on D-Day. We were all . . .
COREN Well, in fact I was go . . .
NERD . . . in dinner jackets, Lord Reith used to insist on that, you know, we had to wade ashore in full fig, and let me tell you, anyone in a made-up bow tie was simply asking to be shot by one of his own men, dinner jacket, patent-leather pumps, white carnations, and, of course, cummerbunds for everyone over the rank of studio manager. Yes, well, as you have pointed out, I was first on to the beach, I had Larry the Lamb on my right, as I recall, Professor Joad and his Harmonica Rascals on my left, and, unless I am very much mistaken, Norman and Geraldo Bones bringing up the rear.

COREN And did you . . . ?

NERD How could I? Dear God, laddie, does your generation of pansy quiz-panellists and cockney newsreaders have any idea what conditions were like Out There? Have you the faintest conception of what it was like trying to get your headphones on over your opera hat with all hell breaking loose around you, E. W. Swanton's Palm Court bloody Orchestra sawing away so you couldn't even hear your bloody cues?

COREN E. W. Stanton? I never realized he . . .

NERD No, well, you wouldn't, people these days don't, that is exactly my point, not of course that Swanton wasn't a great broadcaster, I shall never forget the day we parachuted into Arnhem together, he wasn't with the Palm Court Orchestra by then, they'd all copped it when Jerry bombed World Service, went down like a row of ninepins halfway through *Lillibullero*, he was a ventriloquist after that, E. W. Swanton and Eamonn Andrews, and . . .

COREN Archie, surely?

NERD Oh God, yes, archie, tracer, mortars, they were chucking everything at us, a 20mm cannon shell went right through my spare morning suit on the way down, took away both tails, Reith was *livid*, but poor old Swanton came off a lot worse, dropped straight onto a mine. Still, a great broadcaster, a great broadcaster! Do you know what the dummy's last words were, laddie?

COREN I'm afraid not.

NERD *Give 'im the money, Barney!*

COREN Incredible.

NERD Yes, especially as the dummy had been blown into the next field. By heavens, they could throw their voices in those days, laddie, not like your long-haired atheist layabouts in their scurf-ridden off-the-peg velveteen rubbish who pass themselves off as vents today. *Give 'im the money, Barney!*

COREN What did it mean?

NERD Mean? It meant he didn't have to think up a new joke every week, of course. It was called a catchphrase. Everybody had one. Remember *Can you hear me, mother?*

COREN Who was that?

NERD Dame Myra Hess. Wonderful woman, used to broadcast a concert every week from the Henry Hall, started every recital with *Can you hear me, mother?* Wonderful broadcaster, brought the house down, God know why they put her in Spandau.

COREN Look, I think you may be confu . . .

NERD Probably for not wearing a dinner jacket.

COREN But naturally, after the war, conditions imp . . .

NERD *After* the war? By heavens, laddie, shall I ever forget it, it was the Golden Age of Wireless, you know, but of course, it was the age of austerity, conditions were terrible, I did my first outside broadcast from the back of a wheelbarrow, the 1945 Derby, I had Bert Ambrose between the shafts, God he was game, we were in contention as far as Tattenham Corner! Still, it might have been worse, poor old Uncle Mac drew the Grand National, as I recall. Fell at Becher's and broke his dress-monocle: Reith was all for having him shot.

COREN Yes, I remember Uncle Mac, now I recall he had a catchphrase too, wasn't it *Goo* . . .

NERD Yes, *Can I do yer now, sir?* Exactly, you see how it all comes flooding back, I can picture him now at the Tower Ballroom, Bob and Alf Dimbleby at the organ, it's part of one's heritage, is it not, laddie, it is like the Royal Family, I believe you were just on the point of asking me about the Royal Family, weren't you, you were going to ask me if I had any embarrassing or hilarious experiences during the many years of outstanding royal coverage for which I was both proud and privileged to receive my MBE?

COREN Well, I . . .

NERD It was in the days of the old queen, who . . .

COREN Surely not?

NERD . . . who called me into his office one morning in 1938 and said, 'Look, this is all pretty hush-hush, but the King wants to marry someone called Wallace Simpson,' and I was naturally aghast, and I said, 'Good God, I mean no offence to you, sir, I mean, it takes all sorts, I mean, live and let live, but *marriage*? Can, er, *they* actually *marry*, these days?' and he said, 'That is exactly the point, Nerd, they can only marry if he abdicates, and he is coming into the studio to say precisely that to the nation, will you look after him?' Well, what could I say? I met the King at the door of Broadcasting House, and I took him up in the lift, and just before he went into the studio I shook his hand and I said: 'I hope that you and Mr Simpson will be very happy together, sir.'

COREN God, that *is* embarrassing!

NERD I should say so. The king broke my dress-teeth. I had to broadcast in my off-duty set. Reith was furious!

COREN I can see how he would be. But you were, of course, forgiven?

NERD I have never been certain. I remember wondering, when we all went into the water off Normandy six years later, why I was the only one with his feet chained to a concrete block, but I put it to the back of my mind. One had to: it was what being a professional was all about. The affair simmered on, though— as late as 1951, when I put in for two-and-threepence expenses for a snoek omelette consumed during my all-night vigil on the Skylon and winched up to me in a Force 10 gale which blew off all the chips, Reith sent the bloody Brains Trust round to knock me about.

COREN That must have been . . .

NERD God, they were bastards! Ray Ellington was the worst, you know. But one took it, one was not some jumped-up bearded illiterate teenage oik with a fashionable bog-Irish accent and a place in the executive car-park for his Rolls bloody Royce, was one? One had shared the odd jar down here with Howard Marion Ryan, one had swopped anecdotes with Alvar Milligan, one had spent five marvellous years as a major seagull, privileged to watch great men come and go, carrying their eight records and a Bible.

COREN Good heavens, I had no idea, I had assumed that that was a recording, I . . .

NERD Ludwig Koch could not be everywhere at once, laddie! Many's the time we professionals have had to pitch in when the archive chips were down. Would your Russells and your Kennies and your abominable Noels and all the rest of their mincing unwashed *galère* put *their* hands to the pumps, the way we did? I have been raspberries in my time, laddie, I have been rattling doorknobs, I have been windy nights, I have been feet running on shingle. Once, during the great and heady days of *In Town Tonight*, I was three taxicabs, two newsvendors, and a Number Eleven bus with a severe gearbox rattle! Show me a Terry or a Barry who can claim the same!

COREN Truly wonderful years, Mr Nerd!

NERD Quite.

COREN But then, of course, along came television, and . . .

NERD Oh, really? Did it?

Blue Flics

Six English bobbies are off on a cycling tour of France. They hope to meet the ordinary Frenchman in the street and put across some idea of what life as an English policeman is like.—Daily Express

MONDAY AT 11.42 am, a time which will be corroborated by my colleague PC Garsmold although I did not, of course, consult with him prior to taking down these notes in writing, we disembarked with our regulation machines from the ferry *Sylvia Blagrove II* and proceeded in single file in an easterly direction along the Rue Maritime, in so doing passing several bollards.

After approx. six hundred yards, we come to a roundabout: pausing to ascertain it was safe to proceed, we had just pedalled off when this van came round it the wrong way, hurling PC Chatterjee from his machine, causing severe damage to his left-hand pannier with the result that a mutton vindaloo prepared special by his wife as a safeguard against trots etcetera brought on by, e.g. snails legs and so forth, got scattered all over the road, rice becoming all gritty and dogs jumping on the larger lumps.

The driver of the van then brought his vehicle to the halt position, and descended from it via the passenger door, this detail spotted by PC Wisley and took down by him at the time, 11.53.

The following conversation then ensued:

DRIVER Gabble, gabble, gabble, etcetera.
PC GARSMOLD Excuse me, sunshine, is this your vehicle?
DRIVER Gabble, gabble, gabble, plus arms waving about.

PC WISLEY Leave it out, you was on the wrong side of the road, we have got you bang to rights, also sitting in the passenger seat, definitely.

PC RIMMER Do you reckon he might be intoxicated, PC Wisley?

PC WISLEY I think it is a line of enquiry worth pursuing, PC Rimmer, due to where he is a frog and they are all piss-artists, if I may use the vernacular, get him to blow in the wossname.

PC Garsmold then extracted his breathalyser kit. The suspect then became agitated and, clearly refusing to blow in the bag as laid down in paragraph nine, subsection fourteen, seemed about to offer actual violence. We then employed reasonable force to restrain him, and while he was distracted by the action of picking up his teeth, PC Chatterjee stuck the tube in his mouth.

The test proved negative. We informed the suspect that he was a lucky bastard, and instructed him to mind how he went in future. As we pedalled off, PC Rimmer noticed that the steering-wheel was on the passenger side, and offered the opinion that the vehicle had probably been botched up after some major accident and would undoubtedly not pass its MOT. PC Chatterjee was all for going back and bunging chummy a 703/14b, but the rest of us reckoned he had probably learned his lesson, and anyway time was getting on.

It was now 12.27.

Proceeding through Boulogne, we became aware that everybody was on the wrong side of the road, also using hooters immoderately, but decided to take no further action due to reinforcements not being available.

Reached outskirts of Etaples at 2.07 pm, stopped at roadside to consume sandwich rations. We was on the last of the Marmite when a vehicle drew up, and an occupant dismounted, smiled at us in what might be described as a cordial manner, exposed himself and began widdling in the ditch. He was immediately apprehended by PCs Garsmold and Wisley, and charged with an act of gross indecency. He thereupon twisted himself free, adjusted his dress, and drew a revolver. Since we had not come tooled up, we were forced to lie face down on the verge while the flasher gabbled into a pocket transceiver.

At 2.09 (approx., due to watch-hand clasped behind neck), a vehicle with blue flashing light come up wailing, disembarking a number of uniformed men carrying sub-machine guns. Fortunately, one of these spoke English.

He immediately charged PCs Garsmold and Wisley with importuning.

I then produced my warrant card, and explained the confusion. This decision immediately regretted by our party, since our original suspect then grasped PC Garsmold and kissed him on both cheeks, instantly confirming our first suspicions. We did not take further action, however, due to where they was all armed to the teeth, but it was useful experience. In a country where the poofs go round mob-handed carrying automatic weapons, you have to watch your step.

Tuesday Spent the night at the Hotel les Deux Souris, and came downstairs at 8.00 am for cooked breakfast, just in time to spot landlord pouring large brandy for customer in blue vest.

Two blasts on whistle brought PCs Garsmold and Wisley out of khazi on double to act as back-up while I charged landlord with Dispensing Alcoholic Beverages Contrary to the Stipulations of the Licensing (Hours) Act 1947.

The customer thereupon threatened me with a long cudgel he had clearly brought along for this purpose, and I had no other recourse than to truncheon him. As it fell to the ground, his cudgel split open to reveal several slices of salami and a thing with holes in which I originally took to be a house-breaking implement of some kind but which upon further forensic examination by PC Chatterjee turned out to be cheese.

The following conversation then ensued:

PC WISLEY I charge you with taking away a lavatory with the intention of permanently depriving the rightful owner. You are nicked, son!

CUSTOMER Groan, gabble.

ME To what are you referring, PC Wisley? It is my intention to nail him for assault with a deadly loaf.

PC GARSMOLD PC Wisley is correct. When we was in the khazi just now, we noted that the pan had been nicked, due to where there was only a hole in the ground. It is clear to us that while chummy here was engaging the landlord in conversation over an illicit drink, his accomplice was out back half-inching the toilet. He is probably half-way to Paris by now, wherever that is.

At this point (8.06), the landlord's wife come in to see what the altercation concerned. She was able to reassure me that our friend in the blue vest was above board, also no licensing infringements, so it all passed off amicably enough, us chipping in for bottle of brandy (*see attached chitty*) for customer, plus small sum in compensation for beret. Upon being complimented on her grasp of English, landlord's wife explained she had sheltered escaping English prisoners, which very nearly upset the apple-cart again, due to where PC Chatterjee attempted to do her on a harbouring and abetting charge, since he had spotted someone in the room next door to his who bore a striking resemblance to a notice we'd had pinned up in our section house concerning a bloke wanted for the Lewisham payroll job. He can be a bit dim, PC Chatterjee, but we got to have one or two of them about, these days.

Pushed on towards Abbeville without further major incident, although PC Rimmer, when we were about halfway there down the N40, paused outside a small town and attempted to collar a bloke with a paintbrush for defacing a public sign. Turned out the place was actually *called* Berck.

Wednesday Further to our enquiries, and pursuing our investigations to the fullest extent, we have now formed the firm conclusion that this is a country populated entirely by the bent. At the same time, it is impossible to get a single charge, however reasonable, to stick.

At 9.47 this morning, proceeding down what was clearly High Road, Abbeville, in broad daylight, we come on a couple of wrong 'uns unloading a truck outside a butcher's, to wit,

43

Gaston Dubois. We knew they was wrong right off, on account of they was both smoking during the unloading of fresh carcases, in direct contravention of the Health & Public Hygiene (1953) Act, but we did not know how wrong until PC Wisley drew his notebook and approached said offenders with a view to a sight of their Licence to Convey, which is a technicality you usually nick these buggers on due to invariably being out of date.

The following conversation then ensued:

PC WISLEY (*sniffing*): Hang about, PC Rimmer, does that smell like normal decent tobacco to you?

PC RIMMER (*sniffing*): No, PC Wisley, that is definitely a substance. These men are smoking a substance. That is two cast-iron charges already, and you have not even got your pencil out yet!

PC GARSMOLD Were we to find a half-brick in their apron, that would be . . .

PC WISLEY, RIMMER & GARSMOLD ONE HUNDRED AND EIGHTY!

PC GARSMOLD I'll see if I can find a half-brick anywhere.

At this crucial juncture, however, an even more major crime was detected. PC Chatterjee, who spent some time in the Mounted Division until resigning upon the discovery that the mucking-out was always down to him for some strange reason, suddenly grasped my arm and informed me that the carcase being carried into said Gaston Dubois was that of a horse! I come over dizzy at the horror of this, but quickly recovered due to years of training, and we launched ourselves upon the miscreants firm-handed in the full assurance that there was a Queen's Commendation in this, at the very least.

As for coming out of it with three stripes up . . .

Thursday They finally let us out of Abbeville nick this morning, but only after impounding our bicycles in lieu of surety. It is clear to us that the Abbeville force is unquestionably on the take, probably half a dozen fillet steaks per day per man from Mr Bleeding Dubois, but it is not our intention to stay around long enough to get an A10 investigation going. Sooner we are out of this bloody country, the better.

In accordance with this decision, and machines being in a non-available situation as outlined hereinabove, we was away on our toes double-quick with a view to hitch-hiking back to Boulogne.

It was the first stroke of luck we'd had in four days. At 11.14 am, this big truck stops, swarthy occupant in dark glasses, on his way to Boulogne. We got in the back, and he was off like the clappers.

The following conversation then ensued:

PC GARSMOLD What's in them crates, PC Wisley?
PC WISLEY *Tinned Fruit*, it says on the side. *Export to Mexico*. I'll have a shufti. Could be stolen blouses, anything.
PC Wisley then opened a crate.
PC WISLEY False alarm. Great long pointed tins with EXOCET on the side. God knows what that is. Probably the vegetable equivalent of horsemeat.
PC RIMMER They'll eat anything, the Frogs.

Upon arrival at the Boulogne docks at 2.18 pm, we were at pains to thank said driver for his assistance and informed him he was the first straight Frenchman we had met. He replied that he was an Argentinian.

That explains it, we said.

Shelf Life

HE SETTLED down into the old creaking leather of the club chair on the other side of the roaring fire from mine, and let out a waistcoat button.

'That was a damned fine piece of beef,' he said, cloaking a soft eructation with one tatooed hand.

'I'm glad you enjoyed it,' I said.

'It put me in mind of—' he paused in the thoughtful stuffing of his ochre meerschaum; a flake of dark shag fell on his old mongrel dog; his parrot nodded, drowsing. 'Tell me,' he said quietly, hardly louder than the night wind murmuring at the cottage mullions, 'did you ever eat human flesh?'

I shook my head.

'I don't think so,' I said.

He smiled.

'If you had,' he said, 'you would not have forgotten. It is not, of course, to everyone's taste. Some find it rather sweet.' He resumed the stuffing of his pipe, working his iron hook with remarkable precision. 'But that, as they say, is another story.'

I pushed the Cockburn '97 towards him.

'You were going to tell me,' I said, 'about Muratex Shelving Systems.'

My guest struck a vesta against his whalebone leg, and sucked at his pipestem, his one good and glinting eye vanishing into a cloud of acrid slate-blue smoke. The parrot woke, and coughed, and re-settled. The dog rooted idly in its matted groin. At last, my visitor settled back his head against the chair, took a deep draught of port, half-closed his eye, and began . . .

'Who can say what strange agency first drew me to the benighted spot on the Bristol waterfront that was to be the start of it all? Call it Fate, call it Old Nick himself, call it Mr Witherspoon of South-West Area Sales who had informed me that an estimate was required for a 6 × 40-foot run of executive shelving from our attractive Nobby Nutt range, to be finished in two coats eau-de-nil, plus making good.

No matter, now. Suffice is to say that I presented myself at what transpired to be a deserted warehouse, let myself in, and set immediately to work with what we call a measuring tape, the details of which need not concern us here, except to say that you pull it out, and when you want to roll it up, you press a little button and it sort of flies back.

So absorbed had I become in the problem of whether to secure the stanchions by toggle-bolts or self-tapping coach-screws that I did not notice that I was no longer alone. Conceive, my dear sir, of my amazement when, upon looking round, I found myself face to face with a heathen Chinee who had raised above his head what appeared to be a sand-filled sock!

'So solly,' he murmured, in the manner of his people. It was the last sound I heard. A black pit opened up, and swallowed me.

I awoke with an aching head and a strange motion beneath my supine body. I struggled erect, to find myself in a small room lit by one circular window. It was to this that I now, full of foreboding, ran. It was exactly as I had feared!

Hardly had I taken in my fearful predicament than the cabin door burst open, to reveal a squat and villainous dago, a wild-eyed mulatto dwarf, and a great red giant of a man whom I immediately recognized, from a picture in a recent number of *Shelving News*, to be a full-blooded Pawnee!

The dwarf scuttled forward.

'Bridge!' he snapped.

I smote my forehead, in instant comprehension.

'There has been the most frightful mistake!' I cried. 'I do not play, gentlemen! Since you have kidnapped me to be a fourth, I can only suggest that—'

In answer, the redskin merely tucked me beneath his enormous arm and carried me aloft to the wheelhouse, where he set me down beside a black-bearded ogre in captain's rings.

'Is this the wretch?' roared the captain, and, not waiting upon their reply, reached out, grasped my shirtfront, and dragged me to the adjoining cabin. 'See anything?' he cried.

My trained eye swept expertly about me.

'Dear God!' I breathed. 'All your shelving has crumbled away!'

The captain released me on a sudden, and bit his knuckle.

'Moby Woodworm!' said he, choking a sob. 'All me bits and bobs fallen to the deck. Look at that!'

He stopped, and picked up a pitiful egg-timer cunningly fixed to a tiny Eiffel Tower. Sand ran from the shattered globes.

Mine was, it is true, an unorthodox commission: normally, Mr Witherspoon would have required an invoice in triplicate plus small deposit to ensure prompt attention at earliest mutual convenience, but, as I was quick to assure the captain, Muratex Shelving Systems were usually prepared to waive such requirements in the event of, say, having a cocked pistol stuck in their ear or the ear of any of their representatives.

Working around the clock, I completed my task in less than a week. I was just sanding down and removing dowel-heads as per client's stipulations, when the ship's carpenter entered, admired my work, tore it off the wall, and threw me overboard.

Jealousy, my dear sir, has been the curse of bespoke shelving since Time began.

I cannot tell how long it was before I came round, to find myself bobbing alone in the South China Sea, thanking God that the shelving to which I had somehow remained clinging had been jettisoned with me. Nor had I been troubled by sharks; clearly, shelves are one of the few things these monsters fear.

And yet, sea and broiling sun had taken their own toll. Weak as I was, I should doubtless have perished there and then had it not been for a miracle! As my hands slipped from the trusty dovetailing, I felt a huge, smooth shape rise up from the very deep, lifting me above the water. I clutched wildly, and found a strong fin. I hardly dared glance down; it was a dolphin! I recognized him instantly from a recent feature about marine intelligence in *Cantilever & Bracket Digest*, titled, as I recall 'Dolphins: Could They Hang Fitted Cupboards?'

How long, how far, it towed me, who can say? All I know is that when I was finally released, it was in shallow water; sand embraced my thankful feet. I crawled through the last few warm ripples, and slept.

As to the voluptuous Polynesian maiden who found me there, dressed my wounds, took me to her grass hut, fed me on mao-mao, yuccatash, and succulent hoi, made me a hat, and performed services undreamed of in the letters columns of *Shelving For Men*, I shall not dwell upon her, for the memory, even now, remains too poignant. She called me Nyuga Nyuga, which in their language means Eric, and, during those blissful months, made me forget everything, including my worries concerning the £2 7s 8d already paid into the Muratex Christmas Club that I might never see again.

But such an idyll could not possibly last. Life, my dear sir, is not like that. With the spring came the inevitable invasion from the neighbouring island whose natives, once every hundred years, traditionally give up vegetarianism for Lent. Everyone on my own island was eaten, with the exception of myself: since I alone was white, there were fears that I might have gone mouldy and I was thus taken back to the neighbouring island for scientific tests to determine whether or not I was fit for human consumption.

Having assured themselves that I was indeed edible, the islanders set about sealing my fate. I was tied to a stake, faggots were heaped about my feet, and, while the islanders stood around drinking Campari and discussing what to do after dinner, I prepared to meet my Maker.

The chef approached, torch in hand; the diners crunched

49

their Twiglets, unconcerned; far-off, a gibbon barked; and I, dear sir, I gritted my teeth and swore to myself that I should be as tasteless and stringy as it lay within my power to be!

But at that moment came a sudden high-pitched and echoing cry, to be followed seconds later by a wild and sobbing ululation. I dared not open my eyes as I felt a knife-blade slice through my bonds! What could it be? A sudden eclipse of the sun? An unexpected manifestation of St Elmo's Fire? Had a sliver of glass somehow fallen from a broken compass in my pocket, focused the sun, and set light to the chief's dinner-jacket?

It was none of these. When I finally found courage to look, my eyes fell upon none other than my trusty, if by now somewhat warped, shelving! Washed up at last upon the beach, it had been discovered by the two trembling sentries who now bore it reverently into the centre of the village, pointing from it to me, and back again, before falling to their knees and banging their foreheads upon the ground.

The rest of the assembly immediately followed suit. How this remote island had come to regard shelving as a god I did not know then, and I have not discovered to this day. I was not concerned, either, with staying long enough to find out! Explaining, as soon as the tumult had quietened, by means of sign language and the few local words taught me by my island love, now sadly eaten, that I would have to leave them now to go and put up a fifty-foot run of best pine god in the palace of the great white lady across the sea, I persuaded them to lend me an outrigger canoe and a couple of big strong girls, and, as a silver medal of moon rose over the indigo ocean . . .'

'Yes?' I cried, leaning forward across the dying embers between us, 'Yes?'

My guest rose, sighing, and kicked his dog awake.

'How I discovered the shelf of Prester John,' he said, 'how I journeyed into the bowels of the earth herself to find King Solomon's fabled range of eye-level kitchen units, how I came upon the North-West Filing System, can, I'm afraid,' and here he smiled a sympathetic smile, 'only be recounted to those industrial purchasers wishing to avail themselves of not less than twelve hundred metres of best-quality melanite-coated steel.'

He reached for his Inverness cape and alpenstock, shook my hand, paused at the door, patted the wall, and murmured:

'Look nice there, our Nobby Nutt coat-rack. You won't regret it.'

And then he was gone, into the enfolding night.

Wrap Up Some Red Roses for an Old Lady

Lesbians are having a place reserved for them on a women's committee by Camden Council. It will also select six other co-opted members of the committee, including a black woman, one woman with disabilities, one female trade unionist, and one older woman.

The borough's 101,000 female residents may all vote, but Camden's 85,000 male residents will be denied a say.—Daily Telegraph

I KNOW I do not have to explain the plot of *La Grande Illusion*. This is an up-market book. You have all seen it eighteen times, either on television or in those cramped, tense art cinemas where they do not allow you to smoke. You have all done your Erich von Stroheim impressions, Pentel duelling scar, click heels, two-bob bit falls out of right eye. Vic Oliver without the violin.

Anyway. I should like you to recall the final scene. Jean Gabin (yes you do, face like a dented dustbin, if he was still alive he'd be advertising Cointreau), having escaped from the German prison camp, makes it to the Swiss frontier, neutrality and freedom. He crosses the border, and is plodding away from it through the artificial snow to open a bank account and get his first cuckoo clock, when a shot rings, I think the expression is, out. It has been rung by a sniper on the German side, in both senses, and it is clearly not the first time he has handled a .303 Renoir, since Gabin goes down like a brick, and the screen says FIN. All very ironic, no wonder it is in everybody's Top Ten between *Citizen Kane* and *Battleship Potemkin*; except mine, where it lost on a points decision to *The Three Stooges Go To Mars*.

It is not difficult to work out why I recall it today, always provided, of course, that you have remembered that I live in

Cricklewood, in the Borough of Barnet. Especially if you have also remembered that I am only *just* in Cricklewood: I live at No. 26, My Road (that's all you get, I do not want people coming round with double-glazing on the strength of being a regular reader), whereas No. 18, My Road, is in Hampstead, in the Borough of Camden. I am sixty yards north of the border.

I frequently stroll up to the frontier, and dream. Camden ratepayers get the dustbins emptied twice a week to Barnet's once (there is nothing so diminishes a man in his own and others' esteem as the assumption by his leaders that he will not notice fish-heads hanging about), and when Camden's street-lamps go phut, they're on again next night, possibly in deference to disabled black lesbians who might otherwise walk into something, but when Barnet's go out, the ratepayer's only course is to buy a torch. Furthermore—I have letters on file to corroborate this, the originals, as the saying goes, may be perused at this office—the trees in Barnet only get examined for parasites every two years, whereas Camden's are seasonally coddled, with the result that, while sixty yards to the south Camden's hand-reared greenery flourishes, down in our bit it's like bloody Passchendaele, just a few old stumps waiting to fall over. What disabled black lesbians lean on in Cricklewood for a bit of a breather, God knows; it doubtless accounts for the fact that we haven't seen many about, recently. If we had a few female trade unionists they might have got something done, but they've probably all emigrated south, they are not mugs.

Not that any of his mattered so much until now, I am a flexible soul, I can adjust to feeling my way home in the dark and not being able to provide conkers for my children, nor would I shrink from admitting the very real pleasure there is in nipping up the road at night to stuff black polythene bags of unwanted fish-heads in the Camden gravel-bin, even if you do have to look a bit lively when you get to the bit with the lights on, but all that was before this morning's *Daily Telegraph*.

Camden is getting something very special.

Not, of course, the official representation of lesbians, blacks, the disabled, or the even more deserving trade unionists; one would expect nothing else from a Borough packed to the gunwales with millionaire quasi-socialists chucking the stuff about like a drunken sailor in order to be able to read their butler-ironed *Guardian* with a clear conscience, you cannot sit there in your Queen Anne front window gazing out smugly onto your sodium-lit spotless dustbins and bug-free elms without sparing a thought for those less fortunate, that is all entirely as it should be.

But what are we to make of an authority that is going out of its way to look out for the welfare of the Older Woman?

I reeled when I read it. Clearly (since it is a problem) Camden is teeming with Older Women; indeed, from the statistics of the Borough's sexual breakdown (a term carrying somewhat different connotations in Cricklewood), there could well be something like two or three Older Women to every Younger Man, at least in the more fortunate streets. That is probably *why* there is a problem: a mere sixty yards to the south lies a lotus-land where, never mind clean dustbins, the Older Women are at their wits' end.

There are just not enough Younger Men to go round.

It may well have much to do with the unarguably great wealth of Camden: packed as it is with merchant bankers, company chairmen, millionaire manufacturers, and all the rest from whom pre-eminence in the rat-race demands a heavy price, the Older Men are clearly dropping like flies. The leafy, trashless streets are doubtless jammed from dawn till dusk with gold-handled coffins wending their lugubrious way to Hoop Lane Crematorium, followed in their crêpe-draped Ferraris by really terrific women who are back on the market, yet know not which way to turn.

They told me there was a place like that, when I was young, and I believed them. It was, as I recall, around the time that *Room At The Top* came out, and a whole generation of young men emerged from their local Odeons in a rubber-kneed daze and banged their heads on the wall, flattening their acne, at the thought that Simone Signoret was out there, somewhere.

Not that it would need to be her, of course. In fact, since she was married to Yves Montand, who almost certainly had more to offer than a brown suit from Meakers and a provisional driving licence, she herself was more or less *hors de combat*, however you spelt it. But the possibility of running across someone who wasn't married to Yves Montand was always on the cards.

We asked little: all she needed was a wide mouth, an open car (or vice-versa, I forget), and a private income substantial enough to ensure that A-level revision could be done in the South of France. That she would have sexual tricks up her sleeve to make your ears pop went without saying. This indeed, it was widely accepted, was what had caused her old man to croak, coming as it did on top of a hard day at the balance-sheet; or, at the very least, to be reduced to a broken creature slumped in his Louis Quinze *fauteuil* and staring emptily at his serried shelves of Ming.

That, in direct consequence, she was after it, was beyond all question. That was the main thing about the Older Woman, there was no preliminary mucking about with a fortune down the drain on *Milk Tray* and nothing to show after six months except a thumbnail broken on a spot-welded bra-buckle; with an Older Woman, it was one smouldering glance across a crowded chip-shop and next thing you knew you'd be at it like knives.

That these fairly reasonable ambitions never came true, either for me or, as far as I know, for anyone of my desperate generation, is something with which I have never been quite able to come to terms, unlike syntax, which I find a doddle. Quite simply, there were no Older Women about. Oh, there were any number of *older women*, they were all over Derry & Toms, flat shoes, lisle stockings (the less fetching had one lisle, one surgical), swagger coats with a brass lizard brooch from which the rhinestone eye had fallen, and voices full of the Bakerloo line. Or they could be spotted, early on suburban mornings, following the United Dairies horse with a small tin shovel. Occasionally, one might even see one actually driving a car, invariably an A35 with a busted rear spring, but the likelihood of their making it as far as the Co-op, let alone Cap d'Antibes, was never one to fill the youthful breast with hope, particularly as they generally had an even older woman in the back, coughing. That, beneath their beige exteriors, there were hidden fires waiting to be stoked, is eminently possible, look at Celia Johnson, but we were callow and unsubtle lads, seeking the carmine lip and the fishnet thigh, and when, exchanging a florin for ten Park Drive, our fingers inadvertently brushed the palm of the big wall-eyed number at Finlay's The Tobacconist, we were not moved to lunge at her sagging cardigan and turn the 'Closed' sign round.

Who knows, maybe they were all foregathered in Camden even then, the truly Older Women? Maybe Camden has always been The Older Woman Capital of the World. In any event, that's where they all are now, sixty yards up the road, across the frontier, where the trees are always greener. Is it, then, any wonder that, as St Valentine's Day approaches, I should fancy a basinful of the warm South?

Well, yes. I have just looked up Mlle Signoret's dates, only to discover that, when I first fell beneath her monochrome spell, she was ten years younger than I am now. Yearn though I might to rally to Camden's stirring cry for help on behalf of its Older Women, can I be sure that what they are looking for is Derelict Men?

Truths have to be faced. It is borne in upon me that, even if I were to make a dash for the frontier, the women of Barnet would not be concerned enough to gun me down. As a matter of fact, they wouldn't have to: a sixty-yard sprint would kill me, at my age.

Metamorphosis

We must accept that authorship has become a part of show business. Hype and hoopla, personal appearances on radio and TV, book signings and lunches, are all an integral part of the publishing game. One wonders wryly how a Kafka or a Dostoyevsky would fare under these modern conditions. —New York Times

12 FEBRUARY They come for me very early, perhaps 5 am, I cannot say, I have no watch. After I purchased the scarf, there was no money for a watch. I cried for a long time before making the decision, in the middle of the store in Hothrolnyczy Street, with many people staring at me. They would steal my watch if I bought one. Perhaps they will steal my scarf. Who can say? At nights I dream of the watch. I am wearing it around my throat to keep warm, and people walk by me, and each one tightens the watch one more hole on the strap. I hear the ticking grow louder. My eyes pop out. So they come for me at perhaps 5 am, it is dark in the mean little hotel room, beyond the window London is a black mass crawling with aliens, why am I here, why are they knocking on the door at 5 am?

There are three of them, a publisher in a black coat of very expensive material with a red carnation in the buttonhole, it is as if he had been shot in the left breast, blood wells out; a person in a striped suit and a spotted bow-tie who is in something called public relations, obviously a policeman of some kind, perhaps a government inspector; and a woman who says that she has been assigned to me, who touches my arm with scarlet claws. I am terrified a claw will catch in my new scarf, will pull out a green thread; it will all unravel, and when the last thread runs out, I shall die.

I ask them if there is time for me to vomit, and they all cry har-har-har, and I am bustled out and into a steel lift, and we drop to music, perhaps they wish me to go mad, it would make things easier for them.

They put me into a blue car, the publisher in the front, and I in the rear between the government inspector and the woman who wants to destroy my scarf, and we drive very fast through black streets. I try to scream but my throat is dry. All the time they are asking me about my flight, it is clearly very important, I must have done something wrong on my flight, but what could it have been? I sat in the lavatory holding my scarf all the way from Prague to London, I did not cough on anyone, I kept my passport in my mouth so that anyone breaking down the door would be able to see it and not take me away to kick me for losing my papers, my conduct was exemplary. I did not squeeze my spots.

The car stops at last, beside a cold canal. They are going to drown me like a dog in a sack for something I did on the flight. No, they are taking me into a building. It has giant eggs all round its roof. What is this place? Are they going to feed me to giant chickens?

They hurry me down corridors. My scarf is flying out behind me, it could catch in something, my neck could snap like a wishbone. Suddenly I am in a room filled with lights and cameras, they push me into a chair, they put a microphone around my neck, I am to be interrogated! The interrogators are a girl with a big mouth and a slit skirt, I cannot take my eyes off her leg, *I must take my eyes off her leg*, they will beat me, and a terrible man with a yellow face and tiny eyes who keeps touching my knee, who keeps saying *Hallo, good morning, and welcome, Hallo, good morning, and welcome*, over and over, perhaps he is not a man at all, perhaps he is a robot, he will crush my knee with his steel hand, I wish to vomit.

The robot speaks: 'Hallo, good morning, and welcome to this hour of *Good Morning Britain*, with us now we are very very privileged to have my very very good friend Mr Franz Kafka who is a Czech, and if there's one thing we're always glad to see at TV-am it's a cheque, hner-hner-hner, hallo, good morning and welcome, Franz, tell me . . .'

I cannot hear his words any more, I am staring at the thing

in his hand, it is a clip-board, he has information about me, it is something I did on the flight, it is something I did in the car, the girl is showing more leg, I have to get up, I get up, but my microphone wire holds my neck down, they are pushing me back into the chair, when will they start hitting me? The robot is still speaking '. . . a little excited, and why not, tell me, Franz, are there wedding bells in the offing, are you, hner-hner-hner, leaning on a lamp-post at the corner of the street until a certain little lady . . .'

I faint. When I come round, I am in the car again, we are speeding through wet streets, the government inspector is saying it went well, the girl is saying it was terrific, really terrific, no, really and truly it was terrific, it was a wonderful idea to start screaming and fall over, that is exactly the kind of break a book like this needs, he made a really terrific impact, especially with his eyes sticking out and his cheeks hollow, a lot of old ladies will rush out and buy the book, good, good, good, says the publisher, where is the first signing?

What are they talking about?

They take me to a big store, it is full of books, many of them forbidden by the authorities, they put me in front of the books and my books are among the forbidden books, and men begin taking photographs of me, I am being set up, I am being compromised, I begin screaming again, but all that happens is that the girl says it is terrific, it is really terrific, screaming is now my trade mark, they can do big things with that in the gossip columns. Then a man I do not know pushes something in front of me and gives me a pen and asks me to sign! I refuse to incriminate myself, I break his pen, the man grabs my scarf, books fall, I am being pulled round the shop, everybody is shouting, police are called, I fall on my knees and beg them to beat me about the head, the girl shouts that this is *really* terrific and makes them take more photographs, I pass out.

When I wake up, I am staring at soup. I am at a long table, up on a platform, in some kind of banqueting room, there are a thousand women in big hats at a hundred round tables on the floor below the dais, they are all eating soup but not taking their eyes off me, is this a dream, what is the significance of soup in a dream? I cannot stop trembling. Someone has taken my scarf. I look around wildly for my scarf, I see a sign that says *Welcome to Foyle's Literary Lunch*, what does this signify, are these women going to eat my book, are these women going to eat *me*? I pinch myself, accidently jogging a huge man on my left, he tells me he is an actor, he has written a book which is propped up in front of him, it is called MY BIG BOOK. It has the huge actor's face on the cover. The man on my right then introduces himself. He is the huge actor's son; he is just as huge as the huge actor and he has written an even bigger book. It is called MY BIG FATHER. It has a photograph of the huge actor's huge son on the back. Suddenly, a chicken bone from the soup sticks in my throat. The huge actor is telling a story about his huge son and cannot hear me choking. The huge actor's huge son is telling a story about his huge father and cannot hear me choking, either. I fall forward into the soup, and it is only when the huge actor's huge son leans heavily across me to ask his huge father which of them is going to use the one about their huge cousin in their after-dinner speech that his weight projects the chicken bone from my throat.

After lunch, they both tell the story about their huge cousin. A thousand women laugh and cheer. Then suddenly everyone is looking at me. There is a long silence. At last, the government inspector runs across, and pulls me onto my feet. Clearly, they want me to confess something. I refuse. From the floor, a voice shouts at me to say something.

I tell them that I have a bad chest, that I have an infection of the pleural cavity, that the State has stolen my scarf so that my lungs will be full of phlegm. I show them my handkerchief. There is uproar, women shriek, tables are knocked over, the government inspector and the girl grab me and drag me off the platform, my feet are off the ground. Suddenly, I am outside, I am in the car again, the government inspector is saying 'wasn't that just a teensy-weensy bit over the top?' and the girl is saying 'no, no, *no*, it was really terrifically impactive, it had a really amazing upfrontalism, it . . .' I put my head out of the window, I vomit.

I am in a cellar, it is some kind of broadcasting studio, it is clearly subversive, all the people have beards and sandals and vests with filthy words on, this is not a government broadcasting studio at all, I have been put here to incriminate myself, my head is swimming, a short woman with huge breasts across

60

which runs the legend **LBC WOMEN AGAINST RAPE** drags me into a tiny plasterboard cavity and puts headphones on my head, they are going to bombard me with some form of sonar lobotomizing, but no, a voice is coming through the headphones, a man is saying 'hallo, Frank is it, this is Brian, a long-time listener but a first-time caller, I have not read this book of yours but what I want to know is what are you doing over here, you black bastard, why don't you get back to Praguolia or wherever it is, why don't you climb back up your bleeding tree . . . ?'

I curl up into a ball. They are winning: they have my scarf, soon they will have my sanity, my soul. I am carried out to the car again, this time nobody is smiling, something terrible has happened. I fall to my knees beside the back seat and beg to know what is wrong. They tell me that I shall not be doing wogan. The girl is weeping. What is wogan? They do not tell me, but I discover that it is something Fyodor Dostoyevsky has done. He has been brought here because of his new book *Crime and Punishment* and, during his interrogation, he was, apparently, asked if he would like to sing with the band. At this, he took out his axe and embedded it in the head of his interrogator. Obviously, wogan must be a form of murder.

Tax Britannica

Archaeologists have unearthed what they believe to be the first Roman tax collecting depot to be found in Britain, at Claydon Pike in the Upper Thames Valley. The depot was built around 70 AD, and probably remained in use until the Romans finally left Britain in 408—Observer

GLUTINUS SINUS, Tax Inspector 126 (Upper Thames Valley Collection), drew the parchment-piled in-tray towards him, removed the curling stack, carefully and neatly squared it off, pared a stylus with the small dagger issued for that exclusive purpose by Inland Revenue Stores (Silchester), straightened his little skirt, and nodded.

'Send him in,' he said.

Miscellaneous Onus, his clerk, scuttled sniffing to the fruitwood door, and opened it. An odour of goat and feet and orifice wafted horribly in; through the gap, Glutinus Sinus caught a brief collage of mud-caked beards and hovering flies and khaki teeth, heard, as always, the distinctive colonial undercurrent of scratching, spasmodically punctuated by the plop of targeting spittle. The inspector shuddered. He had been out here too long. They all had.

'Mr Cooper!' called Miscellaneous Onus, into the miasma.

A squat and patchily hirsute figure detached itself from a cackling group who had been engaged in a curious contest from which the clerk had been forced to avert his eyes, adjusted his mangy wolfskin, and loped into the tax inspector's office.

'Shut the door,' said Glutinus Sinus.

'The what?' said the Briton.

Glutinus Sinus set his jaw, and pointed.

'Oh,' said Mr Cooper, 'it's even got its own name, has it? I thought it was just a bit of wall that came open, bloody clever, you Romans, I will say that for you. Door,' he murmured, shutting it with somewhat melodramatic respect, 'door, door, door, well I never!'

Glutinus Sinus sighed.

'Don't butter me up, Mr Cooper,' he said.

'Me?' cried Cooper. '*Me*?'

'Please sit down.'

'I built a room, once, up my place,' said the Briton, dropping to his haunches, 'only we had to climb over the walls to get in and out.'

'Mr Cooper, about your tax-return for the current—'

'We had not cracked the secret of the door,' said Cooper. 'It was beyond our wossname. It must be wonderful, civilization.'

'Mr Cooper, you are a maker of casks and barrels?'

'Correct. Definitely.'

'And yet,' here Glutinus Sinus riffled through the pile of parchment, selected one, flourished it, 'you have entered a large deduction against last year's income for the purchase of new industrial plant, to wit millstones, four, nether and upper. Can you explain this?'

'I have branched out,' said Cooper. 'I do a bit of grinding on the side. Mind you, don't we all, ha-ha, catch my drift, all men of the world, narmean?'

'Branched out?' said the tax inspector, icily.

'Bit slack these days, coopering,' replied the Briton, 'due to introduction of the glass bottle and carboy. Do not get me wrong, I am not saying glass is not dead clever, probably miraculous even, it is what comes of having a god for everything, the Roman god of glass has come up with a real winner, I am not denying that for a minute. All I am saying is, it has knocked the bottom out of the cask business, having a container what does not leak on your foot when you are carrying it out over the bedroom wall of a morning. I have therefore diversified into flour.'

'Then you ought to be called Miller,' interrupted Miscellaneous Onus irritably. 'All this is cocking up the ledgers.'

'How about Cooper-Miller?' enquired the Briton. 'Due to following two professions? It's got a bit of tone, that, my old woman'd fancy being Mrs Cooper-Miller, she would be invited to open the Upper Thames Valley Jumble Fight, she would be asked to judge the Humorous Bum Contest, it could put us right at the top of the social tree.' He smiled oleaginously. 'We could be almost Roman. Uglier, mind.'

'So,' said Glutinus Sinus, 'you are engaged in the manufacture of flour for profit? Why, then, have you made no relevant return for—'

'Who said anything about profit?' replied Cooper. 'Cooper Flour plc is a registered charity, due to where it is distributed to the needy, gratis. It is a good word, *gratis*, we are all very pleased with it, what a spot-on language Latin is, got a word for everything.'

Glutinus Sinus put his fingertips together.

'True,' he murmured. '*Gratis*, however, does not translate as receiving chickens in return for flour.'

'Ah,' said Cooper. 'You heard about that, then?'

'Mr Fletcher entered them as outgoings,' said the tax inspector levelly.

'Yes,' said Mr Cooper bitterly, 'he would. You got to watch him, squire. The plain fact is, them chickens are definitely not income. We do not eat them. They are pets. You cannot count a household pet as income.'

'How many have you got?' enquired Miscellaneous Onus, licking his nib.

'I don't know,' replied Cooper, 'I can't count higher than XLVI. I have not had everyone's educational advantages, have I?'

'With all those chickens,' said the tax inspector, 'you must be getting hundreds of eggs a week. Surely you eat those?'

The Briton narrowed his already imperceptible brows.

'Eggs?' he repeated. 'What are eggs?'

Glutinus Sinus stared at him for a while. The Briton stared innocently back. Eventually, Glutinus Sinus snatched up his stylus, and drew an egg on the back of a tax-form.

'Oh,' said Cooper, nodding, 'chickens' doings.'

'No, no, no!' cried Miscellaneous Onus. 'They're delicious! You fry them!'

'Get off!' exclaimed the Briton. 'Pull this one. I've seen 'em coming out.'

'In that case,' snapped Miscellaneous Onus triumphantly,

'how is it that Mr The Other Cooper is buying them at eighteen denarii a dozen?'

'Search me,' replied the Briton. 'He is probably putting them on his roses.'

Miscellaneous Onus sprang from his stool, waving a document.

'This invoice carries your address!' he shrieked. 'How do you explain that?'

The Briton squinted at it.

'That's not me,' he said. 'You will notice it is signed Mickey Mus. Come to think of it, I've noticed our yard looks remarkably neat of a morning. Clearly this bloke is nipping in at night, nicking our chickens' doings, and flogging them on the side. What a liberty! Imagine anyone stooping low enough to steal droppings. Mind you, you'd have to, wouldn't you, ha-ha-ha, sorry, just my little joke, where would we be without a laugh now and then, that's what I always say.'

Glutinus Sinus grabbed the paper from his aide, and threw it in a wastebin.

'All right,' he cried, 'but how,' and here he plunged a trembling hand into the sheaf, 'do you explain *this*? It happens to be your list of deductible expenses for the year ending April 5, 408, in which you have not only put down the cost of enough protective clothing to dress an entire legion, but also some score of expensive items described as "professional gifts, disbursements, tips considerations, etcetera" which I cannot but—'

'What a marvellous word, *etcetera*,' murmured Mr Cooper, rolling his eyes and shaking his head, 'nearly as good as *gratis*, I do not know how you lot keep on coming up with 'em, no wonder your beneficient and gracious authority stretches from—'

'—take to be the most gross and transparent attempt to evade your dues, not only all this, I say, but also an enormous sum attributed to, where is it, here we are, "the entertainment of foreign buyers". Mr Cooper, do you really expect me to—'

'It is clear,' said the Briton, holding up one massive hairy hand, 'that you have never been up the sharp end when it comes to coopering and/or milling. On the one hand snagging your professional habiliments on splinters, nails, sharp reeds and I do not know what else, on the other coming home of an evening absolutely *covered* and looking like sunnink ritual cut out of a chalk bleeding hillside, you cannot wash self-raising out of a wolf pelt, sunshine, it turns to paste, try drying it by the fire and what you end up with is a flea-infested giant loaf.'

Glutinus Sinus's favourite stylus snapped between his fingers.

'Very well, but what is this entry: "VII formal III-piece gents' goatskin suits"?'

'Nor,' continued Mr Cooper, not pausing for breath, 'can you turn up with your casks at a smart brewer's premises with your backside hanging out. I am, after all, a director of the company. Similarly, going about the countryside upon my unpaid charitable works and doling out flour left, right and centre, I cannot look needier than the bleeding needy, can I?'

Glutinus Sinus licked dry lips, and glanced at Miscellaneous Onus.

'These professional gifts,' whispered the aide hoarsely, 'who exactly is receiving them?'

'You name it,' replied Cooper. 'It is dog eat dog in the barrel game. You got to grease palms, especially with foreign customers.'

'Aha!' cried Glutinus Sinus. 'At last we approach the nub, Mr Cooper, or would you prefer I called you Mr Mus? Just exactly who are these foreign customers of yours to whom you are so generous with bribes and entertainment?'

The Briton smiled.

'As a matter of fact,' he said, 'he is a Roman gentleman, one of my most esteemed business associates, a person of great probity and standing. I am sure you would be the first to appreciate that you cannot fob off such a man with a couple of bags of stone-ground wholemeal to stick under his toga and a ferret kebab up the takeaway.' Cooper picked a dead wasp from his beard, carefully. 'He is my accountant, Dubious Abacus. I understand he is a big gun. If you care to re-examine my files, I think you will discover that he has authorized my tax-returns personally. I do not know how he finds the time, what with constantly running back to Rome to do the Emperor's books.'

After a long silence, Glutinus Sinus said:

'We would appear to owe you a not inconsiderable refund, Mr Cooper-Miller.'

The Briton rose slowly from his haunches.

'I'll see the bloke on my way out,' he said.

After the door had closed, Glutinus Sinus stated at it for a long time.

'What year is it, Miscellaneous Onus?' he said.

'408, Glutinus Sinus.'

The tax inspector sighed.

'Get our suitcases down,' he said.

The Denmark Factor

'KEEP OUT' WARNING TO DANES

By GODFREY BROWN
Agriculture Correspondent
in Brussels

A STERN warning that
B. itain would, if neces-
sary, use the Royal Navy
and R A F in its fisheries
dispute with Denmark
came yesterday from Mr
Walker, Agriculture Mini-
ster.

Daily Telegraph

BLOODY GOOD.

I have in front of me a curling paperback edition of *Tourist In Copenhagen and Northern Zealand*, published, true, in 1953, but it can't have changed much, give or take the odd live show starring Greta The Jutland Superwoman And Her Donkey Sid. Anyway, it's all they had in the local library, they are not yet on a war footing; when that I was and a little tiny boy, with a hey, ho, the wind and the gripewater, the Hampden Square Public Library had two-colour leaflets on squander-bug-tackling and what to do when an incendiary bomb called and how to dig for victory with an uprooted signpost. Green mesh on the windows, too, and free orange juice and Radio Malt application forms on a bandy utility table near the door, under the Help Fill Sandbags poster. Soon as Jerry's first hobnail hit Hampstead Heath, one was led to believe, he would be up to here in pitchforking librarians before he could even get his Lüger unpacked. Thin spinsters they may have been, grey lisle stockings and spectacles made out of wire coathangers, but not one among them who couldn't have crippled a Tiger tank with a hurled copy of *Gone With The Wind* from two hundred paces.

Different, today.

I said: 'Do you by any chance have a decent map of the

Skaggerak coastline?' and a Mohican with a rhinestoned ear, clearly on day-release from the Snotrag Gestapo Oi Band, said: 'You what?' Dear God, and to think I am about to plunge myself into a war to keep England safe for him, come home with a glass eye and a tin fist and doubtless get charged £1.80 for keeping *Tourist In Copenhagen and Northern Zealand* twelve days over expiry date, also 'If this is blood on page 8, sunshine, the whole thing's going up to Head Office, would you mind not leaning your crutches on the window, some of us have got a job to do.'

Anyway, *TICaNZ* has already proved a boon; only half an hour gone and Notty still to creep in front of Camera Four and adjust his upper plate to the grave matters in hand, but here I am with inside dope already stored in the locker. For example, I have learned that the Danish for breakfast is *morgenmad*, a word one might reasonably have expected to mean a sportscar buff, but there you are, it's clearly a tricky language, and the sooner we master it the better, when I burst into the Øplands Gøøse, Helsingborg, spitting grenade-pins at the breakfast-gong and desirous of three streaky rashers, two eggs sunnyside up, fried bread, and mushrooms, if available, I do not want the buggers to be in any doubt as to what I am after. Someone could get hurt.

For we are obviously about to go in hard, and I have no intention of missing out this time. Peter Walker, inventor of the first British cheese for two hundred years and therefore soon, no doubt, to be Lord Lymeswold, is unquestionably a hard-line patriot of the first water, and when he hits the Skaggerak beach bent on overthrowing Danish Blue and all it stands for, I shall be screaming at his shoulder, and you can lay to that. When the Falklands were invaded, I was taking a light breakfast in Monte Carlo with Lord Chalfont, the reasons for which need not concern us here, and I was all for running to a telephone and volunteering on the spot, but it was his considered opinion that it would be all over before the croissants staled, so I naturally deferred to a man who had been in the South Wales Borderers for twenty-one years, resigning in 1961 only to become Defence Correspondent of *The Times* and, subsequently, Minister for Disarmament. Don't talk to me about bloody experts, I could've had an MC by now and two books in the best-seller lists, never mind a safe Tory seat for 1983.

Not that the Next Lot will not be immeasurably preferable to the Last Lot: getting to the Falklands, six weeks on a plain diet of Quells and brown paper bags, would have created all kinds of administrative difficulties, such as putting the cat in kennels and making sure no sits. vac. ads for humorous editors were in the pipeline. Thirty minutes on the hovercraft is all I need for Denmark, if they let me invade in my own car, drive up through Belgium, Holland, and the FDR, and take the swine by surprise in the soft underbelly at Aabenraa on the southern border, which I see from *TICaNZ* has an interesting 18th century church with a 60 m spire. Nip up that and bung a Union Jack on the weathervane, you'd hear Max Hastings's teeth gnashing across four counties.

I shall obviously have to keep a sharp eye out, mind, for Godfrey Brown, stout wordsmith of the extract above. Not only will he be as avid for knighthoods and paperback rights as I, not only will he be spurred by the added incentive of springing, at one bound, from the straw-sucking downmarket rut of agricultural correspondent to the heady status of war reporter, he is also, in Brussels, half-way to the front line already. Given the gung-ho stance of his paymasters at the *Daily Telegraph*, I have little doubt that his requisition-chitty to have his humble Renault 5 given the full rally treatment from turbo-charger to modified suspension is even now winging through the in-trays with all due expedition. I have unfolded the map gummed to the inside-front-cover of *TICaNZ*, and the roundabout at Vesterbrø looks like a good place to run him into the ditch; if they haven't changed the one-way system since 1953, of course.

Strategy is the name of this little game. Meticulous attention to fine detail. God knows what will become of me if the Brussels bookshops carry a later edition of *TICaNZ*, Godfrey bloody Brown could have the first ten chapters of MS at Weidenfeld & Nicolson before I've even found out whether 65 øre is still the rate for an airmail envelope. It was in 1953 (*see p. 15*). Come to think of it, I do not even know what an øre is: you do not hear the word bandied about much when the talk turns to baskets of foreign currencies. Do the Danes still have it, or do they use something else? I could be standing in the Main Post Office at 33 Købmagergade with the greatest length of martial prose since *All Quiet on the Western Front*, it'd do me a fat lot of good if all I could get out of the clerk behind the airmail grille was a hysterical shriek along the lines of 'Støne me, bløke here thinks we're still using øre!'

If the Main Post Office *is* at 33 Købmagergade, these days. It may well be a døner kebab house, by now, or a dispensary for sick animals. Anything.

That, of course, is one of the things that makes Denmark less attractive than the Falklands. It is clearly more complicated. Bone up on kelp and penguins, you've got the Falklands sorted out in twenty minutes. In Denmark they don't even speak English, except, as I recall, at Elsinore, where they do it in iambic pentameters. Put a foot wrong, literally, in Elsinore, they'd have you spotted for an enemy before you'd even got your Bren assembled. You'd be on the wrong end of a poisoned rapier and borne out on a bier in ten seconds flat.

All things considered, it may be better, on reflection, to go in with the Task Force, can't be more than six hours from Harwich on the SS *Lord Matthews*, even if it does mean helping to keep the *Daily Express* going for a few more weeks; war, after all, is about making supreme sacrifices. If I book now, I can probably get a porthole. As I understand it, you get a band playing on the dock and girls from the *Sun* waving their bras at you, it is all very romantic and probably good for a couple of thousand purple words, always provided the Ministry of Defence dobermanns let you get near the ship's typewriter and you don't fall into the fatal trap of pointing out in print that the cost of the war means that you could give every herring in the North Sea £200,000 and still come out in front.

And that's all right by me. I'm sure the Government knows best. She usually does.

Christmas Message

British Telecom is to allow telephone users to make cheap phone calls throughout the Christmas period from December 24 to January 4. 'It is a time of year when people have a great deal to say to one another, and BT rather wanted to enter into the spirit of the season,' said a spokesman. —Daily Mail

'. . . when he come home on Christmas Eve, well I say come home if you can call coming home where there is this noise like scaffolding falling off a lorry due to where they have left their thumb on the bellpush and no one running to answer it on account of I am only their bloody mother, aren't I, and I am up to my elbow in the turkey, you cannot run to the door with a handful of raw giblets, you cannot get turkey liver blood out of deep-pile mushroom carpet, I speak as one who knows, it is not as if it was figured, you do not notice so much with figured carpet, so by the time I have put the giblets in a safe place, I do not have to tell you what comes over a cat at Christmas, it is my belief they put something in up the hormone place where they do turkeys which attracts cats to turkeys, not something a human can smell, it is like them high-pitched whistles for dogs, they put in something out of the range of the human nostril, do not ask me why, unless it is in the hope that the cat will have a go at the turkey while you are elsewhere, for example finding a sprout which has rolled under the fridge, which would mean you would have to go out and buy another turkey, or worse, make do with a goose, they are always trying to offload geese, nobody wants a goose, all fat, you sit there with your chin shining, also leaning over a burning pudding your chin could probably catch light, your whole face could go up, hair, everything, you read about it all the time, mind you that is probably what the bastard wants, it would just suit him if I was to go up in flames, never mind Christmas, he would be off like a bloody shot with one of them big-busted cows in Accounts, it would not come as a surprise to me if he hadn't fixed it with the butcher, he's a devious bastard, he probably read it somewhere, it is probably in Agatha Christie, someone murdering a wife with burning goose fat, it is all he bloody does in bed these days, read thrillers, anyway where was I, oh I know, I run out into the vestibule and the chime things that hang down, I don't know what you call them, they are supposed to do 'The Bells of St Mary's' but they have not been right since we got them, it is possible they went wrong in the post, never order by mail is my advice, apart from anything else they get your name on the computer, it is like Moscow, before you know it you are full of double-glazing and quilted housecoats and people coming round from Social Security to make sure you are not doing the milkman, it can all start with sending off for chimes, I speak as one who knows, anyway they have never played 'The Bells of St Mary's', what they play is a bit like 'Volare', don't remind me about that holiday in Benidorm, all my skin come off, I had to sleep standing up, not that they play anything at all *now*, never mind a bit like 'Volare', due to where they had their thumb on this bellpush God knows how long, these mail-order items cannot take punishment of that nature, they are all made in Korea, they are not built to last, I run into the hall just in time to see one of the chime things come off the wall, right on the cat basket, I put him there when I'm stuffing poultry, lock him in a normal room when there's this hormone smell about, he'll have the paper off of the walls, I've seen him claw through a draught excluder before now, they go mad, well they're jungle animals, really, you cannot entirely civilize a cat, did you know that, he's fourteen and never answers to his own name, well I opened the door and he was hanging there between the big pimply messenger, Norman from Regional Distribution, and a little darky, and you do not have to be Magnus Magnusson to see that they have widdled on the mat, you would think they would have more respect for an eight-pound-ninety-five wreath, never mind three pound on silver bells, it is my considered view that the little darky was behind it, they come over here straight out of the trees, but you cannot say nothing to them, for example why have you weed on my mat you little heathen sod, do you not know this is the birthday of Our Lord, because before you know it they are all round the Race Relations Board due to you being on the computer with the mail-order chimes etcetera, I have known decent people end up in prison over less than that, so anyway, they just dropped my bloody Brian, didn't they, and run off, and I dragged him inside, and right away I could tell, I said what's that smell, and he said what smell, and I said don't give me what smell, you drunken adulterous pig, I may not be able to afford cheap scent out of the miserable bloody housekeeping but that does not mean I cannot recognize it when someone walks into my hall, ha-ha-ha walks, when someone *crawls* into my hall smelling like budget night in a Gyppo brothel, who was it this time, that tall skinny mare from Novelty Gift Vouchers, so he said *that, that*, you mean *that*, and I said yes, I mean *that*, and he said *that* is my new after-shave, that is what *that* is, Mr Bromstone give me that on account of a year's loyal and devoted warehouse management, so I said Mr *Bromstone* give you attar of bloody roses, Mr *Bromstone* give you British Home Stores Numero Bloody Sink, what is he, some kind of pansy, pull this one it has bells on, show me the bottle then, and *he* said after they threw us out of the Rat & Cockle due to where big pimply Norman was sick in the free avocado dip, not so's you could notice afterwards, but never mind that, after they threw us out we didn't have nothing left to drink so we sat in the car-park and drank my bottle of Macho Bigboy, that is probably why I smell so strongly of it, shall I help you do the tree now, and I said you touch my children's tree with those hands what have been God knows where, you desecrate the holy fir, you defile one chocolate Santa, I said, I'll put you in bloody traction, and I do not know what might have happened then if the cat hadn't come by like a bullet with the turkey in its gob, blood everywhere, feathers, due to me not having noticed that when the chime fell on its basket and busted the lid it had took off, straight into the kitchen, straight onto the turkey, I couldn't believe it when it shot past me, for a moment you couldn't tell whether it was the turkey had got the cat, you hear about where they run round months after their heads have been chopped off, anyway they both run upstairs and when I finally got them out of the loft I had scratches all the way up both arms and the turkey only had one leg, also covered with fluff and mouse droppings from the loft floor, it was no good just rinsing it under the hot tap, I found the cat's bell inside it, it had obviously stuck its head up the turkey's bum and had a go at the white meat from the inside, I had to soak it in Dreft, I would not risk it in Ariel, despite superior stain removal, on account of it being biological and bound to react with an artificially hormoned turkey, I have seen them films where after an atomic explosion all the ants come out the size of double-decker buses, I could not go to bed leaving a battery turkey soaking in a biological cleaner, I would not be able to sleep, can you imagine it all swelling up as big as an elephant and hopping about on this one enormous leg in the middle of the night, running about the house and looking for its head, you would not get any help from bloody Brian, either, he would doubtless put it down to a figment of his bleeding boozing, I have seen him when he thinks there's spiders on the wallpaper, I would have to face the bugger alone, it would have the tree over like a shot, fuses blowing, glass balls going off, at least you know where you are with Dreft, I have remained loyal to Dreft and Stork during eighteen years of marriage, they do not let you down, unlike men and children and bloody cats, eighteen Christmases, do you know what he bought me this year, he bought me a five-pound ironmongery token cashable at any branch of Robert Dyas, that is what was waiting for me when I got up on Christmas Day, three hours sleep and the turkey all wrinkled up in its blue polythene bowl, do you want to know what kind of a Christmas Day I had, let me tell you what kind of a Christmas Day I had, it all started with the . . .'

Enigma Variations

A Russian book just published alleges that a 'Sir Edward Pelham Hollis', a senior Foreign Office diplomat, passed secrets to top Soviet Agents working in Western Europe in the 1930s and later.

Diplomatic Service lists of the 1930s and 1940s, however, contain no mention of any 'Sir Edward Pelham Hollis'. Nor is there any record of such a name in Foreign Office registers. —Daily Telegraph

THAT THE name of Sir Edward Pelham Hollis does not appear upon the hallowed rolls of either the Diplomatic Service or the Foreign Office will come as scant surprise to those historians among us accustomed to probing the riddle wrapped in a mystery inside an enigma; an apophthegm, incidentally, coined by Sir Edward himself during his period as a mole with the Churchill Speechwriting Unit and expressly designed by Stalin, it being October 1939, to destabilize British relations with the Soviet Union and thus justify his imminent non-aggression pact with Hitler; a subterfuge completely lost on Churchill, carried away as he was by the ringing appeal of the phrase. The sentence itself, of course, bears all the tell-tale hallmarks of *Roget's Thesaurus*, the book which originally had been so fundamental to Sir Edward's own great deception, even if its influence was not always as successful. Indeed, it was his blunder in penning 'We shall fight them on the beaches, and at the seaside, we shall fight on the sands and on the plage and in the lido, we shall fight on the shingle and on the pebbles' which finally incurred Churchill's irritation and got Sir Edward sacked from the unit and seconded to Naval Intelligence.

But I hurry ahead.

Sir Edward Pelham Hollis was born plain Andrei Andreyovich Korchnov in the small Byelorussian town of Vitebsk, in October, 1907. Like so many of his class, he went to a miner prep school, graduating as a face-worker in the spring of 1923 and going immediately to work in Number 7 Shaft of the Osdnievski Glorious People's Colliery. It was here that the disparate strands of contemporary history fortuitously combined to bring young Korchnov's potential to the attention of the relevant authorities; but to understand why, it is necessary for us to transport ourselves back to those bleak and frugal years of dire hardship which followed upon the Revolution.

Food was extremely short, and the reason that so many young men wanted to go down the mines was that you got to eat the canary. It was, not unnaturally, a crime punishable by death, but there was no way in which the authorities could discover that it had been committed, since miners merely emerged, weeping as Russians will, from the pit, explaining that the comrade canary had dropped dead and had been given a decent non-denominational burial down below.

But Korchnov (as even the layman will have guessed from his subsequent career) was a homosexual, and as such highly unpopular down the mine, where it was often pitch-black and thus impossible to tell who had grabbed whom, with the result that perfectly heterosexual stakhanovites would frequently batter one another to death under the mistaken impression that one of them was Korchnov. Thus hated, he was never offered a piece of canary; whether his resultant course followed from his feeling that he was an outcast of the Establishment, as he later claimed, or from simple hunger, it is at this distance impossible to say, but the fact is that on February 16, 1924, Andrei Andreyovich Korchnov went to the colliery supervisor, blurted out the facts of the canaricide, and put the finger, for the first time metaphorically, on a number of his workmates.

Eighteen were shot. Korchnov was whisked out of mining for his own protection, and sent to work as a clerk in the newly founded OGPU, which, for those unfamiliar with the name, of course stands for Obedinyonnoye Gosudarstvennoye Politicheskoye Upravleniye. Here, the iron continued to work its way in the young Korchnov's soul: the menial drudgery of secret policework was not for him, he longed for the challenge of the upper echelons, the specialized senior work, the hugging, the kissing, the pressed flowers, the slim volumes of Pushkin's verse bound in green calf, the real silk camiknickers, the Max Factor survival kit, the Chanel Number 5 miniature atomizer which was part of every top agent's arsenal.

But it was not to be. Month followed month, year followed year, the 1920s became the 1930s, and still Andrei Andreyovich sat in his drear little cubicle just inside the entrance at the dreaded 287 Pyostov Prospekt, huddled over his boring in-trays and his dog-eared code-books, watching the great ones come and go: tall, elegant, beautifully turned out, laughing gaily, tossing their lovely heads, chatting of Fragonard and Mozart and Rainer Maria Rilke, exchanging anecdotes of punt and choir, just back, perhaps from the Bolshoi, and just going to the Hermitage—Andrei Andreyovich would watch them bitterly from behind his towering files, grinding his cheap tin teeth, hating the undeodorized reek wafting up from his cheap sack suit, wincing at the agonizing tweak of his plywood shoes, and swearing to himself that someday, somehow, he would join that glamorous and distinguished band of heroes who had done so much to put the Mother back into Russia.

But how? He had not even been to England, let alone Cambridge. For him, an Apostle was a painting on wood you ripped out of the local cathedral and bunged on the bonfire when you were incinerating the bishop; for him, an invitation to the Palace meant the chance to pump a couple of rounds into a minor Romanoff; for him Goodwood was the stuff you managed to collect on your half-day off to stick under your basin to heat your shaving-water, and Ascot was the impossible dream of something you stuck on the wall so that you wouldn't have to go out in the snow to collect Goodwood.

Nor, in fact, did he know any English at all, except for a handful of phrases that his heroes, passing his mean little desk and glancing at his pinched and pockmarked face, would giggle at one another, and these he did not understand, though he cherished them; evenings, he would sit in his tiny room, gazing into his sliver of mirror and murmuring, 'Don't think much of yours, ducky!' cursing himself for its tantalizing meaninglessness.

And then, suddenly, in 1934, Fate smiled.

Because of his increasing personal unsavouriness around the office, Andrei Andreyovich Korchnov was put on fieldwork. Somehow, an educated man, an intellectual even, had slipped through the OGPU net and was still alive in a remote Ural village; since Korchnov had been the one to spot the discrepancy in the ledger, his superior threw him the bone of doing the job himself. He drew a length of piano wire from the OGPU stores, and went off to dispatch Doctor Zemolevski.

And it was there, a thousand secure miles from Moscow, that Andrei Andreyovich's million-to-one number came up. For Doctor Zemolevski was not merely an intellectual, Doctor Zemolevski was not merely multilingual—Doctor Zemolevski was actually, by profession, a plastic surgeon!

In the same instant that the flash of inspiration burst upon Korchnov, he slipped the piano wire back into the lining of his moth-eaten fedora. For there was a deal here to be done, and Doctor Zemolevski would do it, if he valued his life and the fresh start among California's sagging matrons that Korchnov's access to the Visa Section could afford him!

So they began. First, the nose, deflated of its Slav bulbousness, nipped, tucked, slimmed, turned up; then the space between it and the upper lip, lengthened to a perfect hint of horseness; then the lips themselves, thinned, yes, but retaining an element of fleshy cherubism, and pouted to highlight the new dimples gouged in the depilated cheeks by Zemolevski's flashing scalpel. And last, the hair, transplanted, crinkled, bleached, so that it flopped breathtakingly over the langorous new lid of one blue eye. It was superb! Even Zemolevski, family man, bound by professional ethics, could not, when the work was done, forbear from planting one small signatory kiss upon the soft new cheek.

Whereupon he packed and left for Pasadena; but not before he had passed the bare essentials of social English to his patient, as agreed, and taken from his library the thesaurus which would amplify those rudiments, and pressed it into Korchnov's new limp hand, along, of course, with those selected introductions to Renaissance painting, Venetian architecture, Restoration comedy, and Donizetti opera, without which the English diplomatic double-agent can never pass muster.

Korchnov sat in the departed Zemolevski's study, slim legs crossed, long fingers clasped over one slightly trembling knee, and pondered a new name. Since Roger Hollis, he knew, was a man destined for high Intelligence office, the surname chose itself; Edward conjured up an image of lush privileged England, of steam yachts and mistresses, of rolling roughshoot. A knighthood was obligatory, to demonstrate both skill and impeccable probity. Sir Edward Hollis, then? Not quite. A touch was needed; and, since as part of his course he had been read to, his face and eyes bandaged, by Zemolevski from the one corpus which, at a stroke, would tell him all he needed to know of the background whence he was supposed to have sprung, a background of dotty aunts and clever butlers and chinless heirs and apoplectic lords and simpering fiancées, that touch was instantly forthcoming in the Master's own first name: he would call himself Pelham.

Sir Edward Pelham Hollis jumped out of his chair, and hugged himself! He minced across to the desk and snatched up the thesaurus, and thumbed it through, seeking to describe his lovely new name.

'It's exquisite!' he cried, shrilly. 'It's delicious, it's delectable, it's stunning, it's simply too, too *divine*!'

And then he tossed back a roguishly wayward curl, shimmered to the front door, closed it gently behind him, and caught the next train back to Moscow.

To A Degree

The Further Education Unit has urged universities to admit self-taught mature students, in a report which states that there is not one college that will admit people with no formal qualifications. Mr Norman Evans, author of the report, has accused those responsible for student admissions of being unaware of 'what adults learn these days without being taught. People learn from friends, radio, television and the press.'—Daily Telegraph

I'M GLAD you asked me this question about *Othello*, number three if you haven't got the examination paper by you, I know what it is like being a professor we are both men of the world, narmean, I saw that thing on television with that, God what was his name, I don't think he did anything afterwards, he was good in that, though, I'm going back, what, could be four, five years, thin little bugger with one of them Viva Chapati moustaches and a striped vest, anyway he was a professor and most of his time was spent in, not to put too fine a point on it, a leg-across situation, it did not look like he got a lot of lecturing etcetera done of a morning, he was never off the nest, so I know how easy it must be to lose examination papers, also screwed up by people lying on them, I trust I do not have to draw pictures!

You can hardly blame him, women these days, I saw in, the *Sun* was it, that only 3% of women over sixteen south of possibly Bolton, could be Bradford, were virgins, it did not specify nuns or similar included, I suppose it would be tricky asking a nun, but they probably keep a register up the Vatican if you really wanted to get to the bottom of it, where was I, oh yes, women these days, it is not surprising dons are getting it by the shovelful, I had a girl in the cab the other day, flagged me

81

down outside Imperial College, two in the morning, I don't stop for everybody then, of course, you would not catch me going through e.g. Brixton with the light on, or Kilburn, they can be just as bad, get four Irishmen in the cab, middle of the night, you wouldn't believe the damage they can do, have you any idea what a cab costs these days, fourteen grand without the word of a lie, this is due to where Mann Overton, their name is, have a monopoly, they can charge what they bloody like, look at it, it's a tin box, is what it is, you could buy a Mercedes 280 for fourteen grand, not that I'd touch a German car, still sometimes you can't help wondering who won the war, have you ever thought about that? God, what was I, oh I know, yes, so this girl, this student, she's in the cab and I'm looking in the mirror, aren't I, and she's got this white sort of a trenchcoat effort on, did you see *Casablanca*, well, like that except no trilby, and I'm driving along and we're chatting about this and that the way two students will, I was telling her, as I remember, about these statistics I heard on the radio, this bloke phoned in to Brian Hayes and it was all about should we sell Russian grain to the Americans on account of all the missiles everywhere etcetera and millions of people starving in, in, in some part of Africa, ended in -i as I recall, and suddenly we're at Sutherland Avenue, I remember all them flatlet houses when they were requisitioned by the Ministry of Food, God, powdered egg, will I ever forget! Anyway we stop at this house in Sutherland Avenue, and I say that'll be four pound sixty, and she says oh blimey, look at me, I have come out without my trousers, i.e. no money, and I turn round and stone me, she has not got a stitch on under the mac, and she says: 'Will this do?'

Know what I said?

Go on, have a guess.

I said: 'Have you got anything smaller?'

Ha, ha! Geddit? Well, bloody hell, Professor, you got to laugh these days, haven't you, or you would go raving mad, that is a well-known medical fact, there was this thing on BBC2, they had that one who's a qualified doctor *and* a comedian, it'll come to me in a bit, was he Monty Python, anyway, for argument's sake, Doctor Python is talking to this foreigner and they are talking about stress, and the upshot was that you have just got to laugh. That was the top and bottom of it. There are these tribes somewhere, and they do not laugh, and they are all in the bin by the time they are thirty.

I think that that is Othello's problem, when you come right down to it, women throwing theirselves at him and him not having a sense of humour. If he had said to Desdemona, for example, have you got anything smaller, I am only putting that forward as a for instance, I am not comparing myself with Shakespeare, but just suppose, just *suppose*, that that was what he said instead of strangling her, they could have had a good old laugh about it.

It could be to do with where he is black.

I think Shakespeare put his finger on it there, I mean he made him black for a reason, right, it was not a question of tossing a coin, it was a decision not to make him, e.g. Belgian, say, or one of your dagoes, he was definitely after a smudge. Could be an idea he picked up off a cab-driver, it is a well-known fact that Shakespeare got about a bit, and if you sat round the shelter of an evening you would find a lot of experts ready to back him up. It is not a question of prejudice, it is a question of coming over here and not having a sense of humour. I'm not saying they all strangle their wives, just some of them, they have different values, life is cheap in the paddy fields, ask anybody, and it is not a matter of who is right and who is wrong, it is just that when an Englishman suspects his old lady of having a bit on the side, he will take it in good part, he will just knock her about a bit and go down the pub. Your black is not quite so civilized, in the literal meaning of the word, i.e. from the Greek for out-of-the-trees, as I understand, so it is not for us to blame the poor bastards, it is for us to keep them off our patch; take Mr and Mrs Othello's kids, they would have been neither one thing nor the other, I saw this *World In Action* where they have a terrible time, personally I blame Desdemona's father, when Othello come round he should have told him to sod off.

Basically, where Question Three goes wrong is in putting it as: *What is the tragic flaw in Othello?* It is not *down* to him, he cannot help himself fancying a white woman, it is in their blood, they do not think of nothing else, it is a well-known fact;

if you are looking for tragic flaws it is down to the rest of them for not putting him straight right at the off. I realize, of course, that a line like, e.g., 'Right, Othello, on your bleeding bike!' in the middle of Act One might alter the wossname, structure, a bit, but you could always beef up Iago's part, he could step in and then you would have a play about him and Desdemona, I don't know, running a pub or going into the oil business or deciding to grow all their own food in the back garden or something, it could be a series, there is no chance of a series if you strangle the bloody heroine at the end of the first episode, am I wrong?

Part of the trouble was making him a general, of course, instead of a bus conductor.

There is another flaw in the play, I don't know how tragic you'd call it but it certainly sticks out like a sore thumb, a number of people I was discussing it with up the betting-shop noticed it straight away, it is that nobody in it smokes. There are, what, twenty characters in it, give or take, and none of them ever lights up or offers a packet round, it is definitely a flaw. According to statistics, six adults in every twenty are regular smokers, and there they all are, talking away for hour after bloody hour, and nobody fancies a drag. As you know, I have been to a number of lectures on Elizabethan drama, and there's a lot of rubbish about sources and figures of speech etcetera, and in my view that is one of the troubles with universities, not seeing the wood for the trees. It takes people from outside to notice, and while we're on the subject, has it struck you that nobody in *any* of Shakespeare's plays, never mind *Othello*, goes out for a widdle?

Strange, but true.

Funny thing, and I'll go on to Question Four in a minute, don't worry, I've got a lot to say about Milton and his silly bloody ideas about people, it's easy to see Milton was never in the army, I'll come back to that, but I'd just like to point out this funny thing, if you'll bear with me, I had this bloke in the cab the other day, tall man in one of them long overcoats with the fur collar for catching the scurf in, a senior executive of some kind I suppose you'd describe him as, and I thought to myself: your face is familiar I thought, I've seen that face somewhere before, well, you have to have a good memory in this business, Professor, you would not believe what people leave behind in taxis, shoved down the seat or even, pardon my French, under the . . .

The New Extremely English Bible

Most Britons still believe in the concept of sin and nearly a third believe in hell and the devil, according to the biggest survey of public opinion ever carried out in the West.

Britons have a stricter moral code than their fellow Europeans on serious sexual, criminal and social matters, but they are more permissive about minor infringements, such as failing to report accidental damage to a parked vehicle.

The Observer

From Genesis 3 et seq.

9 And the LORD God called unto Adam, and said unto him, Where *art* thou?

10 And he said, I heard thy voice in the garden, and I was afraid, and I hid myself *amongst* the trees of the garden, because I *was* naked; and I was in fear lest thou shouldst ask of me whether I had *eaten* of the tree of knowledge.

11 And the LORD God spake unto him, saying: never mind eating of the tree of knowledge, thou hast walked on the grass of knowledge, for a start.

12 And the man said, I thought it was all right to walk upon the grass of knowledge, I did not know that that was any big deal.

13 Whereat the LORD God *waxed* exceeding wrath, crying: There are signs up everywhere. As to thy *being* naked, thou art not naked at all, the LORD thy God hath eyes in his head, thou and the woman *that* I made for

thee have picked leaves to be a covering, what dost thou think thou art playing at, picking things, it will be the daffs next. 14 And the man replied in thus wise, saying, The woman whom thou gavest *to be* with me, she hath done this. I was happy in my nakedness, it was not draughty, but the woman insisted, and I plucked of the tree two leaves, contrary to *subsection* eight of the by-laws, para fourteen.

15 And the LORD God said unto the woman, What *is* this *that* thou hast done? And the woman said, The serpent beguiled me, saying it would be fashionable, a smart leaf.

16 And the LORD God grew great in his anger, crying, It will be riding bloody bicycles on the footpath next, It will be failing to put sweet wrappers in the receptacles provided; and he turned then to the man, saying, Hast thou a licence for this snake?

17 And the man fell upon his knees in *that* place, shouting: licence, what licence, it is not a dog, it hath no legs, it doth not bark, wherefore is it *that* I should have a licence?

18 But the LORD God would not be assuaged, saying, I know it is not a dog, I the LORD thy God made it, it is not an elephant or a plaice, either, do not get clever with me, the fact is *that* it is a dangerous animal within the meaning of the Act, they can kill you, snakes, I speak as one that knoweth, and as such they require a licence obtainable at any post office that I have made.

19 And the man hung *his* head, saying, I did not realize.

20 But the LORD God exculpated him not, saying, Ignorance of the law is no excuse, *it is* not even on a lead, it could foul the footpath, they are no joke, snake droppings. This is the garden of Eden, not an adventure playground.

21 Therefore the LORD God sent them forth from the garden; and he placed at the east of the garden of Eden Cherubims, in caps and armbands, and a flaming signboard *with* all the by-laws writ large upon it, to keep the way of the tree of life.

4 And Adam knew Eve his wife; and she conceived, and bare Cain, and said, I have gotten a man from the LORD. 2 Whereat the LORD God spake unto them, saying, I trust *that* thou hast registered this child, also that thou hast registered him once only, I do not want any maternity grant fiddles, I do not want him

coming back *unto* me when he is unemployed claiming two lots of social security, I give thee fair warning. That could well be a matter for thunderbolts.

3 And she again bare his brother Abel. And Abel was a keeper of sheep, but Cain was a tiller of the ground. And in the process of time it came to pass, *that* Cain brought of the fruit of the ground an offering unto the LORD.

4 But the LORD God was greatly displeased in that place where he was, saying, Call that a tomato? It is more like a red pea, hast thou no thought for the Weights & Measures Act *that* I have made, dost thou turn thy back on my Office of Fair Trading, what is it that thou art trying to put over on the unfortunate public?

5 And Cain replied in thus wise, saying, Public, what public, there is only we and thou in this place where we are, thou hast not built a public yet, unfortunate or otherwise.

6 And the LORD God gathered up the clouds and spake to him in thunder, crying, Do not take that tone with me, I am the LORD thy legally constituted local authority, a thing is not a tomato unless I say it is a tomato.

7 And Cain went away in anger from that place, saying, It tasted all right, what difference doth it make if it is a bit undersized, how can you make a living in this business if you do not bend the rules a bit. And lo, he came upon his brother Abel in a field, and Abel had *with* him where he was a sheep that had found favour with the LORD in that it had complied with all regulations concerning weight, quality, vaccination, smell, and all the rest, and Abel said unto his brother Cain, How didst thou get on with that titchy little tomato?

8 And Cain rose up against Abel his brother, and slew him.

9 And the LORD said unto Cain, Where *is* Abel thy brother? And he said, I know not: *Am* I my brother's keeper?

10 And the LORD replied in thus wise, saying, thou art his next-of-kin and it is therefore thy legal obligation to report his demise to the Authorities, especially in view of the fact that it is thou that hath demised him.

11 And Cain said, He got up my nose.

12 And the LORD God replied, saying, That is no excuse for failing to report his death. Coming on *top of* thy dreadful infringement of the tomato regulations, this is too much. And the LORD set a mark upon Cain, reminding

him of the severe penalties involved should he receive two further marks in a period of three years, *under* the totting-up procedures.

13 And Cain went out from the presence of the LORD, and dwelt in the land of Nod, on the east of Eden.

14 And Cain knew his wife; and she conceived, *and* bare Enoch: and he builded a city, and called the name of the city, after the name of his son, Enoch.

15 And the LORD God waxed furious, crying, didst thou get planning permission for a city? Look at it, it hath no proper drains, it hath high-rise blocks stuck up all over *the* place, it doth not have a decent road from one end to the other, it is an eyesore and an affront.

16 And Cain answered the LORD in some heat, shouting, This is not Green Belt, this is bloody Nod, it is thou *that* stuckest me here in this place where I am to be a developer on account of not being allowed to *follow* chosen profession, to wit, tiller of ground, how am I to earn an honest bob, all right, fairly honest?

17 But the LORD God would not countenance his appeal, and knocked the city down, that it be a lesson and a guide to all men.

18 And Enoch, the son not the city, *begat* Irad; and Irad began Mehujael; and Mehujael begat Methusael; and Methusael begat Lamech.

19 And Lamech took *unto* him two wives: the name of the one *was* Adah, and the name of the other Zillah.

20 And the LORD God waxed really spare this time, what with the multiplicity of spouses and the serious begetting explosion, for the infringements were beyond number, and the LORD God *was* up to here with paperwork. And of the myriad thousands that now *teemed* upon the Earth, the vast majority did not make full and complete tax returns, nor did they come home from work without paper-clips and rubbers that they had taken, saying, Who is it that will notice? Also, they lived together in council accommodation when they *were* not legally married, and they did not observe the yellow lines that the LORD their God had laid down for them, nay, not even the *double* yellow lines; and they smoked in those places where there were signs clearly exhorting them not so to do, and built on room-extensions in cedar wood and in laburnum wood and in sandalwood without informing the Rating Authority; and

they sang in those places which did not have a licence for · singing.

5 And God saw that the wickedness of man *was* great in the earth, and *that* every imagination of the thoughts of his heart *was* only evil, continually.

2 And the LORD said, I will destroy man whom I have created from the face of the Earth; for it *repenteth* me that I have made them, they cannot be left for a minute, I am losing a thousand gas-meters a day, never mind forged Cup Final tickets.

3 But Noah found grace in the eyes of the LORD.

4 And GOD said unto Noah, The end of all flesh is come before me; and behold, I *will* destroy them with the earth. Make thee an ark of gopher wood. And this *is the fashion* which thou shalt make it *of*: The length of the ark *shall be* three hundred cubits, and the height of it thirty cubits.

5 Thus Noah and his sons fashioned them an ark; and it was done.

6 But when the LORD God looked upon it where it was, he waxed practically out of his mind, crying, Is that the gopher wood that I commanded thee?

7 And Noah answered in this wise, saying, Not exactly, it is more your actual chipboard, I was very lucky, it fell off the back of a cart, also no VAT, nudge-nudge, catch my drift?

8 And GOD caught his drift, saying, Nor is it the three hundred cubits *in* length, that I bespoke unto thee.

9 And Noah replied unto him, saying, Right, right, there are no flies *on* thee, O LORD, it is about, what, two hundred cubits, give *or* take, it was a pretty small cart if thou knowest what I mean, it looks like bad news for the dinosaurs and the unicorns, one way and another.

10 And the LORD God retreated into the cloud, and wept. And the tears became rain.

Royal Slice of Bread

THESE ARE difficult days for a daddy.

All I can do is enjoin you not to believe all you read in the newspapers. To my virtually certain knowledge, my pert, curvaceous, outgoing, yet at times shy and homeloving daughter Malvolia, twenty-two, has not been up to anything with anyone of Royal birth. I do want to state this categorically now, before the press are all over our premises and ruining her career as chanteuse and novelty soubrette before it even takes off. It is not just Malvolia, with her lovely long legs and firm thrusting young voice, who might suffer, too much attention could also deeply upset her agent, naïve and biddable Nat Rappaport who, if he saw pressmen and West End producers milling around The Elite Theatrical Agency (No Job Too Large Or Small) at 43 Denmark Place, W1, could become extremely distressed.

His convenient proximity to Piccadilly tube and the several bus routes that stop outside his door, to say nothing of the fact that you cannot move round there for vacant cabs, means that poor Nat could be a prey for every Tom, Dick or Harry who fancied a scoop. That is the trouble with being so close to Fleet Street, I and lovely natural ash-blonde Malvolia have told him a thousand times, but will he listen?

Indeed, the whole reason I have decided, today, to break silence in these pages is to scotch the ridiculous rumours before they get out of hand; and I wish I could. The problem is that Malvolia, despite her three O-levels, is such a secretive person. When I asked her point-blank last night, having waited up until 3 am to see whether I should be able to identify the famous face glimpsed in the rear seat of any chauffeur-driven police-escorted limousine that might have been dropping her off after she and her illustrious escort had danced half the night away at Wimps, newest find of the international jet set, when I, as I say, asked her point-blank if the cameras had caught her sharing an intimate moment with any rakish good-looking descendants whose name might not be entirely unfamiliar to close Sandringham-watchers, she merely tossed back her fashionable Gerard Avener bob, flashed me one of her most captivating smiles, and, her smart Caroline Charles blouson flapping, dashed coquettishly up the expensively Duluxed staircase of our elegant yet comfortable double-fronted detached 1930s residence in the much sought-after Tudor style, exuding respectability from every pore at 32, Samarkand Road, NW9, a quiet tree-lined backwater now thrust willy-nilly into the harsh glare of international publicity.

The rumours which, unfortunately, could break at any time have also deeply upset my dear wife, Wanda, forty-two, herself still a highly photogenic beauty and a woman with a bizarre and chequered past whose own story may never be told, as we both feel that not even the *Sun* would dare to buy it, some of the names involved being so famous that, surely, no circulation surge could possible be worth the risk of giving offence?

What—since you ask, and have the public's right to know— it is that has so upset her is that should this story, whatever it is, break, it may no longer be possible for her to hold on to her unique and exclusive store of personal photographs.

Because many of these, both in colour and black-and-white, show gorgeous music-loving fast-car fan Malvolia growing up—from winsome, cuddly, gurgling and entirely unclad nine-month-old baby romping on a tigerskin rug, right through to winsome, cuddly, gurgling and entirely unclad twenty-two year-old chanteuse and novelty soubrette romping on a tigerskin rug, in her first movie, the yet-to-be-released Raincoat Video re-make *Emmanuelle With The Wind*—pressures on my dear wife to release these precious mementoes in the public interest may, she fears, prove too great.

I know how she feels. I empathize. We are a close-knit family. As Mrs Alice Cresswell, fifty-seven, just along this leafy, typically English street, told me only this morning: 'I had no idea anything like this was going on, if it is. You Corens have always kept very much to yourselves. You have always seemed just like us. I often pass the time of day with you. I frequently see you cleaning the car and so forth, just like normal people. This has come has a bit of a bombshell, if it has, I don't mind saying. I believe you are something in the city, though I do not like to pry. This is not that kind of a neighbourhood.'

And the main reason I empathize with still-lovely Wanda, who shops at Waitrose and plays off twenty-four, is that I myself may have great difficulty in weathering the imminent storm, if it accidentally breaks. Because, as the Editor of a great national, nay, international magazine, I am compelled to earn a few bob on the side to make ends meet, mainly to avoid such headlines as GOLDEN GIRL MALVOLIA'S FATHER IN BEAM ENDS SITUATION, should we ever do anything to excite Fleet Street's interest.

As a result, I also run a small double-glazing and loft conversion company, SNUGFITT KOSYKORNERS LTD, which is doing quite nicely, thanks to never being undersold, also all materials guaranteed virtually Scandinavian and coming direct to you from P.O.E., no middleman raking off fat profits and thus generous benefit returned to purchaser, how do we do it? By offering good old-fashioned British craftsmanship, is how. And the plain fact is, if talented busty Malvolia has been enjoying anything Royal on the quiet, the resulting unwelcome limelight could turn my enjoyable little business into a boom industry, with all that that entails. Overnight, orders flooding in to Snugfitt House, 2a Pondicherry Buildings, Harlesden, NW10, could multiply a hundredfold, never mind people jamming the switchboard on 965 0012, especially those ringing from out of London who have remembered to dial the prefix 01.

And where should I be then? Millionaire's Row, is where, with God knows how many worries about vandals scratching the Roller and whether the butler is nipping into the azalea arbour with the second underfootman instead of polishing up the silver *épergnes* in time for dinner with the in-laws, well you know what *she* can be like when she spots a bit of tarnish staring at her across the Beluga, not that it will necessarily *be* her, that is just by way of an example, plucked at random, please do not quote me, it is far too early for stunning grey-eyed Malvolia to make up her mind, she has her career to think of, fat Hollywood contracts will be pouring in at any minute.

Not, of course, that she couldn't do both, whatever those might be, I have always felt that Grace Kelly's early retirement unnecessarily cut off a fair few bob at source, you cannot just sit there opening cats' homes while your old man is up in his helicopter, that way stagnation lies.

Mind, it is not up to me, nor to peaches-and-cream complexioned chess-player Malvolia's cheeky little brother Hector, fourteen, a typical grubby yet endearing English schoolboy, and no mean soccer-player, whose present craze— you know how kids are!—is posing with his loveable mongrel Patcn, or Spot, or something, for any photographer willing to cough up the price of a Big Mac. His mother and I have tried, God knows, to knock this habit out of him, but, well, boys will be boys, I suppose, though why he has to do it leaning against the wall of St Justin's School For Boys, Jan Smuts Crescent, NW9, I'll never begin to understand.

No, it is all up to lissome clear-skinned Malvolia, whose unique and incredibly successful diet should, I feel, one day be written down so that other girls could have her pimple-free and fatless chances in life; at £2.95 or thereabouts, a paperback like that could bring happiness to millions. It is up, I repeat, to Malvolia to choose.

After all, it's her business.

Lif' Dat Bail

The assumption that cricket was an English invention, let alone a white man's one, is utterly erroneous. A form of cricket had been played in Africa for centuries before the European came, and it was from Africa that the game we know today was exported all over the world. —Drum Magazine

THE VERY word *cricket* is, of course, itself of orig, uncert., of etym. dub: the best bet is Swahili, the likeliest connotation sexual, perhaps to describe an organ, perhaps the act of deploying that organ, who can be sure? Possibly a small noise made during. Certainly, the other semantic arcana have their seedy origins in unsavoury sexual puns: *gully, short leg, long stop, over*, for example, may still be found in virtually pristine use along the Lourenço Marques waterfront—'You want gully-gully, mister? You want short leg-over, very clean, you want nice long stop?'—and the fact that *googly* and *Chinaman* are synonymous comes as no surprise to the experienced stoker, for whom, in a lonely port, they unfortunately amount to the same thing.

No fixed date, obviously, can be established for the beginning of the modern game, but most experts agree that it had its origins on slave plantations, where cotton and sugar workers, to relieve their wretched lot, would get up crude matches using a cotton-boll and a whippy length of sugar-cane, the boll being *bolled* at three pieces of implanted bamboo in an attempt to *knock down de wicked*, since the game was also deeply steeped in the fundamental religious beliefs held by the unfortunate slaves. The simple homiletic message of the early game is, of course, clear, and those origins retain their echo today in the name of the spiritual home of cricket, Lawd's.

Gradually, after the American Civil War, the game grew more refined. The slaves, naturally not able to afford the sophisticated equipment in use today, improvised with what-ever they found lying around the battlefields of the defeated South: the small cannonball, for example, introduced the hard missile to the game, the musket-stock replaced the sugar-cane and ushered in the characteristic bat-shape, and very soon, teams of freed slaves were touring Dixieland and playing improvised games against local sides to the delight of dancing, drunken, finger-snapping crowds, whose modern counterparts may be observed today, from the Lawd's Tavern to the Hill at Sydney.

It was probably at around this period that the name stuck. There is no contemporary record of exactly when and how this happened, but the romanticization of the incident in the film *The Birth of the Blues* (the story of the first Oxford vs. Cambridge Match) is probably fairly close to the truth. In that, you may recall, the young English undergraduate (C. Aubrey Smith), while on a visit to South Carolina, notices a group of slaves playing the grounds of his host's ante-bellum mansion, and calls one of the *bollers* over to him with the words:

'I say, boy, what do you call that stuff?'

To which the young black (Stepin Fetchit) replies:

'Why, boss, we calls it cricket!'

Within a very few years and with the increasing mobility of the newly-freed negro, cricket moved off the plantations and into the towns around the Delta. Hardly surprisingly, it was not yet received into the best circles of society, so that many young cricketers learned their trade playing in the brothel districts, like Storyville. The madames found that waiting clients would drink more if they had a cricket match to watch, and for the unemployed young negroes, this was a Godsend. This is from an interview with the distinguished old batsman Jelly Roll Hammond, recorded by Alan Lomax:

'Ah fust started messin' wid a bat when ah wuz in de Gravier Street Orphanage. Cricket wuz a way of keepin' us kids off de street. Ah din have no formal trainin', an' even to dis day ah still cain't read a scorecard, but that din make no never-mind, ah jes' picked up dat ole bat an' ah impervised. Pretty dam' soon ah foun' ah could handle tricky stuff like de short risin' ball outside de off-stump etcetera, an' one day after ah hit 134 befoh lunch agin de Big Eye Louis Sutcliffe Hot Seven, dis high yaller butter-an'-egg man come up to me an' he say "Ah like de way y'all play dat stuff, kid, how's about y'all come to work on mah groun' staff?'' Turnout he wuz just de top ponce east o' Memphis! Pretty soon, ah wuz playin' out back o' De Square Leg Cat House, Noo Orleans, ten dollars a match an' all de gully ah could git, heh-heh-heh!'

The reference to the Hot Seven is particularly interesting. In the early days, teams were very small: Satchmo G. Grace, for example, started off with only five—himself at cover, Kid Ponsford at deep fine leg, Blind Lemon Bosanquet at silly point, and Baby Hobbes behind the stumps. Bunk Larwood had to boll continuously from both ends. But he soon found that this basic ensemble was too restricted, and the team was implemented by two more players, the most important addition being a slow-tempo boller to relieve Larwood at the other end. After six bolls were bolled, Satchmo would cry: 'We'll take a break now, folks!' and Mezz Titmus would come on and send down his off-spinners from the other end. This traditional cry was soon replaced with 'Over!', partly because it was shorter, but mainly because the lewd overtones made the crowd fall about, particularly if it had been a maiden.

By the end of the Great War, white men had begun to take an interest in the new game: not only did cricket move up from the Delta towards Chicago (a fairly direct result of the Volstead Act and the enormous boost it gave to the drinking with which cricket spectators have always been associated), but the first travelling team was formed. The all-white Original Dixieland Test Eleven arrived to play in England in 1919, but the tour was a complete fiasco: the rudimentary English game was played according to very different rules, and the local variations in pitch and rhythm entirely defeated the ODT XI. They found the bunny hop and the turkey trot totally unplayable, and after three or four ill-attended matches they packed their bags and returned to Charleston.

In Chicago itself during these Prohibition years, black cricket still dominated the scene. It was the era of the giants, and consequently of the legends: of men like Wingy D'Oliviera, who had lost his right arm years before in a car crash, yet still became a great all-rounder, hitting a double century against the Mound City Jug Cricketers and, in the same match, taking 6 for 40 with his tricky one-arm-round-the-wicket leg-cutters; of men like Miff 'Sobers', whose nickname derived from his habit of getting through all-night net sessions on two gallons of moonshine and then being carried out to the middle on the following morning and hurling down his murderous bouncers at batsmen whom his captain had told him had signed the pledge. Sadly, his career came to an abrupt end when, in 1926, he killed both opening batsmen for the Temperance VII, and received a 10-30 stretch in Alcatraz on a Murder Two count. However, his brain was by this time so befuddled by alcohol that he went to his prison grave happy, still believing that his final figures had been 10 *for* 30.

And who amongst us who love the game will ever forget that other great nickname, Clarence 'Pine Top' Close? Perhaps the finest silly mid-off ever, certainly the dumbest, Close fielded so short that batsmen were terrified to hook, for fear of breaking their bats on his forehead. Of all the wonderful anecdotes about Close that have become enshrined in cricket's annals, perhaps the one nearest to the spirit of the man concerns the match against the Fletcher Hendren Big XI, played at the Metropole Oval in a thunderstorm in 1929. Just before tea, Close was struck by lightning, losing nine teeth, and immediately cried: "how-zat?", believing he must have caught the ball in his mouth.

And then there was Bix. Leon Bismarck 'Bix' Washbrook, star of the famous 1930 movie *King of Cricket*, hero of Dorothy Baker's fine book *Young Man With A Bat*, Bix was the first white cricketer of any stature, so poor that he often walked out to the wicket with his bat behind him to hide the holes in his flannels, yet so rich in the affection of crowds that as soon as each ball left the bowler's hand, the pavilion would rise as one man, and shout: 'Oh, play that thing!'

He died, at the height of his powers, in 1931; but for lovers of the man and the traditional game, this tragedy was lessened by the knowledge that cricket was now taking a road he would have hated. The Swing Era had begun, and with it the rise of the Big Teams. For vulgarization and commercialization had struck the great game; to attract vast crowds, ignorant crowds, managers were now including anything up to five or six swing bowlers in their huge sides, not to mention dozens of crude sloggers, simply to appeal to the lowest common crowd denominator. Finesse, subtlety, originality vanished; the improvising solo player was no more. The boring pattern of short-pitched balls and haymaking hooks ruled supreme: Artie Bradman's XXXV, for example, beat Benny Hutton's All Stars at Carnegie Bridge in July 1937 by 164 runs, all of them wides. As for Glenn Ramadhin and his endless, worthless search for innovation, it almost ruined the game altogether with its culmination in an ensemble of eight wicket-keepers, four seamers bowling in harmony, and sixty-two men in the offside trap.

It was left to the caring black man and, oddly, the old-fashioned English amateur, to drag cricket back from the brink and remind it of its roots and true genius. On the one hand, virtuoso players unconcerned with wealth and mass-appeal emerged (Coleman Bailey, Lester Lindwall, Thelonious Spofforth), and the small team reappeared (the Modern Cricket Quartet, the Zoot Laker Trio Plus Two); and on the other, in bumpy fields behind quiet English pubs, keen village sides started to come together under Humphrey Compton and Cy Dexter and Ottilie Martin-Jenkins to revive the traditional game. Crude they were, yes and unsophisticated, often pitifully derivative; and yet, travelling the country in broken-down Dormobiles and playing to enthusiastic kids for rent-money, it was cricketers of that brave kidney who kept the old game alive, and, indeed, still do.

As to its future, who can say? Cricket has come a long way from the African slave ships and the chain-gangs and the cotton plantations, and the roads have not always been smooth nor the conditions clement. Once more it is undergoing a somewhat fallow spell, and there are those Jeremiahs, as there have always been, who say that this time it may not recover. And yet, surely, as long as there are sassy kids about, the tough little Fats Bothams, the plucky young Meade Lux Gowers, prepared to grab a boll and an old piece of sugar-cane and an advertising director from a cigarette company, does any of us really believe that this great game will ever die?

Subordinate Claus

IT WILL have come as a grief to many but a surprise to few to learn that Prince Claus of the Netherlands is back in the bin.

As experienced dykewatchers will recall, there were several occasions during the past year upon which the unfortunate consort was crated up and shipped to Switzerland, in the somewhat nineteenth-century hope that this would put the roses back in his cheeks, but all these were, clearly, to scant avail. For this week, the rubber doors of his alpine bolt-hole yawned yet again.

Why Switzerland? We might well ask. It may, of course, be that his Rolex needs repairing, too, and the Dutch exchequer wishes, in these constrained times, to kill two birds with one ticket, it may be that there is some arcane reciprocal agreement between the two countries to swop top gloomies at a substantial discount, it may be that his Dutch GP is dottier than he is, but whatever the reason, the Swiss have bagged him once more, while all the world wonders. Because while the Swiss are unquestionably dab hands at manufacturing drugs, this being where the big money is, what the average Swiss doctor knows about the actual science of medicine you could stick in your eye, provided you were prepared to go elsewhere to have it taken out again. I speak as one with an extensive knowledge of Swiss medical practice, having once broken a thumb in Brig, only to be set upon by nuns armed with analgesic suppositories, which, while they may produce an unsavoury frisson among my freakier readers, are, I have to tell you, much less fun than a homely splint.

Not that Prince Claus has anything so mundane as a busted thumb. What he is suffering from is depression, a disease which admittedly can be so serious as to preclude even me from bouncing jokes off it, but which in his case, so we have been reliably informed, is not so acute as to persuade the Swiss to take his shoelaces away or insist upon a rubber spoon for his morning muesli. Prince Claus is just extremely miserable. As those who saw the *Daily Mail* photographs of his Christmas holiday will remember, he is in what we para-medics call a long face situation. He stood a little behind the rest of the party, leaning on his ski-sticks, and giving the impression of a bloke who has just dropped his last guilder in the snow.

That everyone else in the photograph is beaming fit to melt the piste not only makes matters worse, throwing poor Claus's melancholy into bas-relief, it also drops a strong hint, in my expert view, at the root of his condition. But let us not rush into out diagnosis.

There are, of course, a vast number of background factors that have contributed to producing a psychological seed-bed fertile for the cultivation of misery, not the least of which is the fact that what Prince Claus is consort of is the Netherlands. Even those of us who love Holland would be hard put to make a case out for its capacity to startle and delight. Physically, it resembles Southend at low tide; it is entirely bumpless, so that anyone wishing for a change of view has to go and get the kitchen steps. For the immigrant Claus George Willem Otto Frederik Gert von Amsberg, whose parents really do seem to have gone to the most hysterical lengths to emphasize his provenance, Holland must have come as a fearful let-down after the cheery undulations of his native Germany. Get up in the morning, draw the curtains, and all there is is sky with a thin khaki strip at the bottom relieved only by the odd distant excrescence of a windmill, turning very slowly and gloomily, and going creak.

Indeed, being wrenched away from that native Germany itself, with its variety, its sophistication, its excitement, its marching, must have, over the years, caused him many a pang of *heimweh*. Rushed from school in 1944 straight into the Army must have been immensely thrilling for the aristocratic youth, and while you can take the boy out of the Wehrmacht, you cannot take the Wehrmacht out of the boy. How indescribably depressing it must be now to have all those wonderful uniforms, ceremonial swords, honorary colonelcies-in-chief and all their bright concomitant decorations, and not be able to shoot at anything! You have the kit, and rank, the clout to take the Sudetenland back, but the reason you're all dressed up is to stand behind the wife while she welcomes President Bongo prior to his riveting three-hour after-dinner speech on Dutch-Gabonese tariff agreements.

I shall not even mention Dutch food, probably the most leaden in the world and only two cheeses, indistinguishable from one another in the dark, but what about the cycling? Could anything be more calculated to lower the spirits of a high-born *Junker* than the constitutionally-enshrined requirement for him to get on the royal Rudge and pedal about in the sleet, smiling at oiks? You do not even get drop-handlebars, and, Holland being what it so depressingly is, nor yet the fun, albeit minor, of changing gears. It might, of course, be argued that the omnipresent threat of a ruptured dyke adds at least something of a zest to Dutch cycling, but my personal view tends to the exact opposite, since there can surely be little more calculated to increase endemic depression than the thought of standing up to your waistcoat in the North Sea and wondering whether your dynamo has fused.

Indeed, the whole flavour of accessible monarchy must bring an alum shrivel to Claus von Amsberg's aristocratic tongue: all the longueurs and tedia and duties of the notional summit, yet none of the awe and fawning, it is like being the Archbishop of Tel Aviv. And it is here, at last, that we heave to alongside the diagnostic nub; though it may well elude his smart Swiss shrinks, who will doubtless fill the backs of their ready chequebooks with all sorts of doodled tosh about potty-training and seeing his dad in his underwear, it shall not escape us who move in the real world where the chocolate bars are flat and the clocks don't shout at you. For you and I know, do we not, that what is making Prince Claus chew his lower lip and stare into the middle distance is the fact that he is not Top Banana, but Second Fiddle. Moreover—I shall not say *worse*, for these are liberated times and even the WVS offer karate classes—he is second fiddle to a strong woman.

And the English, I do believe, know a bit about that.

Not, of course, that the Dutch themselves don't. As far as being low man on the totem pole goes, Prince Claus has two immediate predecessors who might have given him pause for thought before he dropped to his knee and fiddled for the affiancing solitaire. Many of you will remember Queen Wilhelmina. How many of you remember Duke Hendirk, who shared her throne for nearly forty years, or, at any rate, stood behind it looking cheesed-off and gazing out of the window? Another German, coincidentally, and one whose subordinate role to the Iron Lady also scarred him with despondency and oblivion, the two being inextricably entwined. And what of his son-in-law, the subsequently-to-be Prince Bernhard, and, stone me, yet another German, born to be Bernhard Leopold Frederik Everhard Julius Koert Karel Gottfried Pieter, Prince of Lippe-Biesterfeld, yet doomed to commend himself to posterity as the bloke who ripped off the World Wildlife Fund and got his hand caught in the till, a course which, as it transpired, he himself blamed on the dominating and domineering Queen Juliana who kept him so permanently under her thumb that the rain collected in his cranial dent. Can we forbear to forgive him for dipping into the gravy reserved for panda and duck-billed platypus, when the threat to their species paled, beside his own, into insignificance?

And so we come to the hapless Claus, sipping his sanatorial Bovril and watching the sun go down on the Jungfrau and himself. His misery is bound to be yet deeper than his predecessors', since this is 1984, when just about the only thing that is getting stronger in this declining world is The Women. Does even the most sexually democratic of us, among which number I unquestionably count myself, not choke back the tiniest sob at the sight of poor old Denis stumbling along behind, struggling pitifully to hold his trilby on, as the PM strides across Goose Green with the wind managing only to make her hair look more Medusan, and the very mines praying she will not crush them under-heel?

Tell me, what do you recall of Mr Meir, or Mr Banderanaike? Give me just the name, nothing more, of Indira Gandhi's husband. Jot down a note or two on the spouse attached to Iceland's steely Vigdis Finnbogadottir—did you even know that there *was* a Mr Finnbogadottirshøsband?

For a truth is there, for all who care to heed it. Which is that strong men tend to include their women—we know about

103

Eleanor Roosevelt, we know about Clementine Churchill, we know about Mamie Eisenhower and Eva Braun and, God help us, Nancy Reagan; but strong women exclude their men. That this is because it enhances a strong man's aura to be seen to enjoy the support of a good woman, but diminishes a strong woman's aura to be seen to be supported by a man, may be only a quirk of prejudice, but it is no less unsettling for that, in view of the increasingly feminist road ahead, for a man tangled up with such a mate.

It is, sadly, a lesson that probably comes too late for Claus. Having shared the bed of a strong-willed Queen for so long, he could well be stuck in the bin for a very long time to come. If he'd only been content just to sit on the end of it for a few minutes and ask for a fag, he, like Michael Fagin, would be out by now.

For Fear of Finding Something Worse

Eccentric, yes, emotionally repressed, possibly, yet courageous, resilient, cunning, ruthless and tender by turns, both passionate and aloof, fiercely loyal, sometimes funny, sometimes maudlin, religious, the English nanny did more to forge the influential men of England than any other single factor. It will be a generation before we truly discover exactly what we have lost with her passing. —The Lady

MY FIRST nanny was just Nanny. I never knew her real name. Perhaps none of us did.

She joined our household in that soft autumn of 1939, when I was scarce fifteen months old, an engaging toddler, I am told, much given to projectile vomiting and opening frogs with a rusty hacksaw blade to get at their hopping mechanism, a practice from which nanny very soon weaned me by the cunning little trick of batting me with a fence-post whenever the gin was on her.

My parents never interfered. My father was just Father. I never knew his real name. All I knew was that he was something in the City. Every morning he would go off in his silk top hat, his astrakhan coat, his high button boots, and the white stick he had purchased as a hedge against conscription. My mother, the younger daughter of the Earl—he was just Earl, I never knew his real name—would then, having thrown his pyjamas after him and slammed the door, retire to her boudoir and address herself to the needlepoint which was her passion. I hardly ever saw her, but from time to time, during the day, one would catch sight of the little embroidered *toiles* she would slide under the boudoir door, showing men in various stages of amputation.

My early upbringing was left to Nanny. Nanny doted on me. She had, I later learned, like so many of her generation lost her only true love in the Great War, a nursing sister who had run off at Mons with a Prussian dragoon who had broken into her tent in search of something to wipe his bayonet on. After the Armistice, they opened a delicatessen in Bremen, from where, every Christmas, Nanny would receive a small ochre *knackwurst*, tied with a pink ribbon, but no message. With the outbreak of World War Two, this *tendresse* not unnaturally ceased, and Nanny's first Christmas with us was, in consequence, a very dark time. She drank heavily, and brought home the worst kind of waitress from a number of ABCs.

Doubtless, it was from her that I caught my deep and abiding hatred of the Hun. Every morning, for example, as she walked my perambulator in Hyde Park, she would suddenly jam on the brake and hurl herself into the ack-ack gunpits, laying about her with a small yet weighty cosh and frequently rendering several gunners senseless, on the grounds that they had shot nothing down the previous night. The Military Police never pressed charges, however, preferring to incorporate Nanny's forays into the Royal Artillery's training schedules, since there was no greater test of the men's alertness. Eventually, the battery was compelled to set up a Lewis gun beneath the Achilles statue, in the hope of bringing Nanny down before she crossed Park Lane, but she could jink faster than a wing three-quarter and the closest they ever came was to blow off my rear wheel and put three rounds into Panda.

By now it was the spring of 1941, and we were unhappily forced to leave London, partly because of the Blitz (our house was struck on three consecutive nights by shells from Hyde Park), but mainly because the military authorities had grown suspicious of my father's disability since, whenever a siren sounded, he would take off at top speed, dragging his unfortunate guide-dog behind him, and threshing his way to the head of the shelter-queue with his luminous cane. So, in early May, with my father now in a ginger beard and his two legs enclosed in lengths of guttering which he would tap fiercely with his pipe, crying, 'My God, I'd teach those Nazi swine a thing or two if only I had my pins!', we left for the peace of rural Hampshire.

Nanny did not accompany us, preferring to bivouac on

Hampstead Heath with a pitchfork in earnest hope of a German invasion, so, at the age of three, I was introduced to Nanny Phipps.

Nanny Phipps was what I believe is termed 'the salt of the earth', a bucolic Catholic fundamentalist who considered Pius XIII a Lutheran bolshevik. It was she who inculcated me into religion by waiting for me in dark corners of our rambling rented parsonage and sandbagging me with a four-pound crucifix. She would then drag me to the bathroom and baptize me by total immersion in a tub of fresh blood, recounting as she did so, in an undulating Wessex chant, the parting noises of some of the more mutilated martyrs. This took place every night during our first three months of residence, only coming to an abrupt end when two inspectors from the Ministry of Food, spotting the mound of slaughtered lambs which by this time had risen above the encircling privet, called at the house on suspicion of black marketeering.

Unfortunately, upon hearing the bell and spotting the official van through the lancet of his attic bolt-hole, my father, fearing the press-gang, panicked, knotted his sheets together, abseiled down the rear face of the house, and set off on his rigid gutter-pipes across the fields in a terrible clanking lurch. I watched him go from the wall opposite my nursery window on which Nanny Phipps had hung me by my wrists for mortification, powerless to help or follow. Crows rose, cawing, as he hurtled jerkily across the dwindling furrows. I never saw him again.

A load seemed immediately to lift from my mother's shoulders. Freed from the nightly trudge up the let-down ladder to the fortified eyrie where my father, according to Nanny Phipps, waited, crouching on the wardrobe, to pierce her with the forked tail common to his infernal kind, my mother now tripped about the premises, singing. Nanny Phipps herself, having been thrown into Holloway on several counts ranging from treasonable butchery to maliciously wounding a health official with a sharp instrument, to wit, a censer, she was replaced by Nanny Widdershins, a great, plump, apple-cheeked, rosy-nosed, white-haired, cottage-loaf of a woman, always smiling, always with a joke on her lips, even when force-feeding me tapioca down a rubber tube or

107

shaking me awake in the small hours to see whether or not I had wet the bed. To this day, I cannot see a chicken crossing the road without either throwing up or ruining my trouser-leg.

Since my mother had always wanted a daughter, and Nanny Widdershins had always wanted an airedale, these two, freed from the constraints which my vanished father might otherwise have put upon their fancy, now had their way with me. Dressed in a velvet frock and false ringlets, I was led around the house on a leash; when other four-year-old boys were learning fretwork and football, I was taught how to crochet and retrieve. Indeed, at the 1943 Cruft's, only a technicality (spotted at the last minute, and in a fashion I shall carry with me to the grave, by a large borzoi) cost me Best Of Show. But Mother and Nanny Widdershins were good sports; they laughed all the way back to Hampshire.

All good things, however, as one learned so often in the nursery, come to an end. In the bleak midwinter of 1944, even as Patton and von Runstedt hurled themselves upon one another in the Ardennes Forest, so Mother and Nanny Widdershins locked wills in a no less bitter battle. I fell sick, and could not crawl out of my basket: Mother diagnosed chicken-pox; Nanny Widdershins insisted it was distemper. Doctors and vets fought it out with bare knuckles on the gravel drive; times were hard, fees were few. How it might have ended, who can say? For, as the altercation reached its height, a camouflaged Hillman Minx swung suddenly into the drive, disgorging four burly redcaps who flung themselves upon Nanny Widdershins, manacled her to the front bumper, and charged her with desertion.

She protested in vain; the more hysterical her shrieks, the more convinced the MPs became that here was but one more pusillanimous metamorphosis of the notorious blind cripple who had eluded them for close on five years. Even the ultimate appeal to reason, at the sight of which even the older vets blenched, was summarily dismissed on the grounds that there were no lengths to which a treacherous swine like that would not go to avoid serving his King. The khaki Hillman shot out of the drive; the medical practitioners sheepishly gathered up their scattered bags and bottles, and slunk quietly away.

As for Mother, she thenceforth gave up the parental ghost.

Unable, on her own, to cope with a growing boy given to singing 'The Good Ship Lollipop' in a breaking falsetto and biting postmen on the ankle, she promptly answered an advertisement in a Salisbury tobacconist's window and despatched me to Miss Sadie Himmler's Academy For Strict Discipline, at which I presented myself the following Monday with my tin trunk and jumbo packet of Spiller's Shapes. Miss Himmler, though initially somewhat surprised, took me in, since I had brought a term's fees in advance, in folding money. A kindly soul when she was not thrashing middle-aged businessmen with her rhino whip, she was good to me, even if I did not fall precisely within her professional remit, and I was happy there, learning much at her fishnet knee. Indeed, as a middle-aged businessman myself now, I still travel down to Salisbury to visit her, though just for old time's sake, now that arthritis has sadly sapped her magnificent right arm.

And what of those early years themselves, and the proud procession of magnificent female authorities that moved so memorably through them? Did they indeed make me what I am today? Who, at such distance, can categorically say?

I know only that when I step into my polling booth next time around, there will, for me, be no alternative.

Bleeding Hearts

Twentieth Century Love Letters. Edited with an introduction by Marina F. Ellsworth—Strathclyde Free Press 492pp £12.50

THUS FRANZ Kafka, writing on November 18, 1920, from Vienna:

'I love you. If you can find it within you to disregard the cold sore on my lip, my left eye which of late seems to have taken on a strange sliding motion all its own, and the peculiar acrid smell not unlike ill mice which I think we both now know has nothing to do with my herringbone overcoat, I should like to believe that you might come, eventually, to care for me, just a little. I ask no more than that. Your devoted Franz.'

An odd letter for a man to write to his hat-stand? Not according to Dr Ellsworth. As her penetrating introduction adumbrates, the poignant letters which follow tell us much about the emotional and sexual dislocations of this bizarre century when, in the choppy wake of Freud, the romantic imagination was not so much liberated from old modes and constraints as shackled to new ones. Kafka, for example, decided to take up with his hat-stand only after his waste-bin, in his view, had turned him down. A curt note to the latter, written just two days before the one quoted above says it all:

'Do you write? Do you phone? Do you acknowledge I even exist? I waited two hours outside Hofmeister's Laundry last Monday in freezing sleet, and you know what my chest is like. I thought we could maybe take in the new Harry Langdon at the Roxy, but did you show up? Goodbye.'

As Dr Ellsworth's annotation of this letter reminds us, it was not easy finding girls in Vienna if you were a Czech with a bad cough and no carpet. Let us not condemn Kafka too hastily.

110

Hemingway's, from a different culture and a different malaise, was another case altogether. All Hemingway's love letters were written to his taxidermist, Adolf Waters, though not directly:

'Dear Butch,' he wrote on 18 July 1928, 'are you ready to stuff the big tarpon yet? He was a good one, he was one of the best ones, I ran him eight hours and he threw every trick there is. It has been three weeks now, and I still wake nights, in that time when there are no clocks striking which is about the worst time there is, and I can still feel the big tarpon through my hands, pulling on the line. I would like to be there when you do the thing with the sawdust. It would mean a lot. Papa.'

Adolf Waters is an old man now, but when Marina Ellsworth went down to his retirement home in Fort Lauder-dale, there was one point on which he was as clear as he was unshakeable. In the late spring of 1931, Ernest Hemingway went through a form of marriage with a moose's head. Adolf Waters has particular cause to remember this incident, since not only did he put the glass eyes in the bride, he was also the best man.

'We found an old drunk JP down in the South Carolina bayou, and he performed the ceremony for two bottles of Jack Daniels. Ernest and the head went off in Ernest's old Hupmobile to the Adirondacks. It was a short honeymoon, but I think they were the happiest four days of Ernest's life. While he was in Spain in '39, the head got moth. There was nothing I could do. Hemingway was never the same afterwards.'

The letters are not all literary, by any means. Dr Ellsworth has cast her net wide to set the century in amatory perspective. A curious little note, for example, from Henry Ford to Madame Louise Dunlap of Pontchartrain house, new Orleans, written early in 1909, speaks volumes for the contemporary mood of the energetic young country:

'My dream is for a popular good-looking woman at around thirty-five dollars, tops. She would be cheap to run, but built to last. Quality control is very important: a man who had one in Poughkeepsie should be able to walk in off the street in San Diego and get exactly the same item down there. And any colour, as long as she's black.'

Or this, quoted in its entirety on page 138. It is a letter

written in Hitler's own hand, in early 1934, and was found among his posthumous detritus:

'I miss you. I need you. I want you.'

According to Bundesarchivist Klaus Bagel, the envelope bore the single word *Sudetenland*. There was no stamp, but a solid body of evidence to suggest it was delivered personally.

Not, I suppose, unsurprisingly, many of the English offerings betoken an altogether quieter, more restrained, more infibulated love, particularly when its expression emanates from that stratum of emotional gentility which is so peculiarly, in every sense, ours. Take this not atypical little Valentine, written *c.* 1931, from a young John Betjeman:

> *Each day in Croydon High Street*
> *I watch my darling pass,*
> *By catching in Boots window-pane*
> *Her image on the glass.*
>
> *She stops; I turn; I tremble!*
> *Shall I reach out my hand?*
> *Too late! She glides on, humming now,*
> *Past Meredith & Bland.*
>
> *Her poignant perfume lingers,*
> *Electric, on the air—*
> *O! Dare I catch her up in Penge*
> *And gently mount her there?*

As perhaps the only love letter ever written to a 28 tram, the item has a certain arcane charm, but do we not feel *nationally* let down, as it were, by the fey delicacy of the passion? Too often this is the temper of the English inclusions, and when it is not, then the alternative is hardly more engaging: a sort of gruff, grudging recognition of a relationship, as if the sender were embarrassed at the display of emotion incumbent upon him. As, for example, this farewell note interred with the remains at a small private ceremony by Evelyn Waugh (who, of course, kept a carbon of everything) so clearly displays:

'Goodbye. You were a bloody fine pair of brown boots, all in all.'

112

According to Dr Ellsworth's footnote, the loss of his boots was what triggered Waugh's conversion to Rome, but this, I'm afraid, is an uncharacteristic lapse into speculation by so punctilious a scholar, since I myself was told by the late Tom Driberg that Waugh's need for a framework in which to endure grief was in fact occasioned on that dreadful day in November 1925 when his best friend ran away with Waugh's first umbrella.

Oddly, Driberg himself has not been included in this collection, so his long and fascinating correspondence with Praed Street gents continues to remain in holograph until such time as some adventurous publisher is prepared to allow the wider world a glimpse into this remarkable relationship between man and porcelain.

One English relationship, however, which I for one could well have done without eavesdropping is the highly unsavoury one-way epistolary traffic from D. H. Lawrence to his *inamorato primo*. I certainly do not intend to dwell upon it in the pages of a family magazine, and would not have mentioned the matter at all were it not necessary for a critic to correct an editor, since once again the eminent Dr Ellsworth nods. There *is* a precedent for someone sending pressed blooms to another part of his body; half a century before D. H. Lawrence enclosed forget-me-nots with his distasteful *billets doux*, a distraught Van Gogh was sending his ear sunflowers, albeit over a far greater distance and thus with rather more justification.

Let me turn, instead, to a much more charming and witty exchange. In 1922, a young English actor left this country for Hollywood; as Dr Ellsworth explains (Appendix XII), he was, like most former boarding prep-schoolboys, deeply in love with the contents of his nursery, his teddy, his rubber-sheet, his nanny's birch, and so forth. In consequence, he took these and other items with him to his new country, where they were never replaced in his affection, even by the succession of nubilia that later came to fill, albeit unsatisfactorily, his Californian bed. Rumours—naturally enough in that wacky, wonderful town—abounded, so much so that a showbiz columnist commissioned to profile the star finally, in 1953, sent him the now legendary telegram: 'How old carry-cot?' and received the equally famous reply: 'Old carry-cot fine. How you?'

Twentieth Century Love Letters, then, is a volume as entertaining as it is informative, a labour—if you will forgive the pun—of love, as well as a work of impressively committed scholarship. If I have one cavil, it is that perennial complaint: no index. Readers, dear Dr Ellsworth, like to cross-refer: an entry under say, *wallet*, would enable us to compare and contrast the letters of J. Paul Getty and Terry Wogan, one under *chamber-pot* the innermost feelings of Benny Hill with the *cris-de-coeur* of Jean Genet and William Burroughs.

But this, as I say, is a minor objection. *Twentieth Century Love Letters* is a volume which no true book-lover with a sense of life's passionate priorities will want to be without: the weight, the feel, the subtle yet heady smell, the, oh God, the handsome binding for you to examine in your own home, the crisp crackle of the spine as you ease it open, the funny little way its delicate pages respond to the trembling finger, the hint, here and there, of . . .

Somebody Up There Like Me

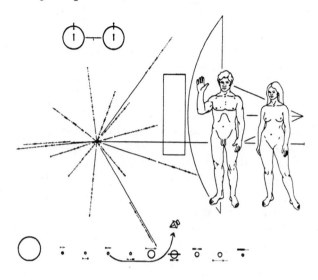

ANYONE WHO knew me in the days when I was a free-floating polymer blob will tell you I'm a changed man. Taller, more shoes, all that. Even those who remember me in later years, as a sixty-foot fruit-eater covered in trim triangular slabs and sporting a rather fetching rockproof ruff, would pass me in Fleet Street today with hardly a second glance.

I have come on a bit, since then.

Nor need we go that far back in order to launch this particular little poser. Why, it is scarcely three million years, if the good Professor Leakey is to be believed, since my fun-filled time in the Olduvai Gorge, loping from hummock to hummock and wondering whether my ground-grazed knuckles were Mother Nature's way of telling me it was time to try something a little more erect. Four feet tall and a parting right down the middle of my back—goodness me, if my friends could see me now!

Look at the poignant little sketch above, and prepare to catch my drift. You will, I know, have already recognized it, since it is as engraved upon our memories as ineradicably as it is upon Pioneer 10: it is Mr and Mrs Man, or as *Guardian* anthropologists might have it, Ms and Mr Woman, stark naked and off on a mission to embarrass the more prudish inhabitants of interstellar space. For, just a short while ago and amid the falling tears and popping corks of Houston, the happy couple broke from the constraints of our backyard solar system and set off on their illimitable wander.

Free, white, and twenty-one, as it were. I'll come to that later.

They were gummed to Pioneer 10 a long time ago, of course, in 1972, when it first found lift-off. This probably explains the somewhat dated hi-tech Habitat-austere furniture on their patio. It probably also explains the fact that it is the man who is saying hallo to the things out there; today, twelve years and a whole heap of raised consciousness on, they would both be saying hallo, otherwise Congress would bow to feminist pressure and take the money back.

Just shows you how far we have come in twelve years.

And do you know how long Mr and Mrs Man are going to be out there on their intergalactic Grecian urn, forever panting and forever young? 'Scientists have estimated Pioneer's *shortest* possible lifetime at 2 billion years,' according to *The Times*. The italics, as they say, are mine. Two thousand million years is how long they're going to be out there, at the very least; however, 'moving through frictionless space, where the chance of collision with another body is so remote that it is beyond imagination, Pioneer 10 could continue its journey to infinity.' I did not bother bunging in any italics that time; if a thing is beyond imagination, it is certainly beyond mere typesetting.

Not, mind, that every aspect of the matter is beyond imagination, else I should not be buttonholing you today. For it is clear that an outside chance exists of Mr and Mrs Man bumping into something between now and infinity, else NASA would not have thrown good money away on Benvenuto Cellini Jr. You know the kind of rigorous scrutiny the poor souls come under, there is always some interfering busybody trying to make out a case for feeding Ethiopia or curing cancer rather than sending a tin postcard into the unending void.

So, then: we are presented with the very remote possibility, but a possibility nonetheless, that sometime in the next infinity or so, an intelligent thing from out there will hear a bump in the night, if they have nights, and go downstairs, ditto, and find itself facing the picture in question. If they have faces.

Now, let us first trim assumptions, for the sake of space. This space, not that. Let us not go down that road which starts with the reflection that the thing out there—could be a smart flower, could be a sapient gas, could be a god in a shower of gold—will take one glance at the figures and not recognize them as Earthlings at all, but as, what? A trade mark, perhaps? After all, thinking along NASA's cockeyed lines, if you sent a Mercedes-Benz into outer space, might not the welcoming committee on, say, Betelgeuse assume that the inhabitants of Earth were all three-pointed stars?

No, let us give the designers the benefit of the enormous doubt and accept that when the inhabitants of some unimaginably distant speck takes his eye out of his pocket and examines the NASA plaque more closely, he will jump to the immediate conclusion that here is a snapshot of that nice young couple from across the universe.

Fine, fine; first hurdle successfully negotiated.

You have, I would guess, already picked up my scattered inklings about the second hurdle. We shall not even go so far as to say that all this is happening at the minimum-survival limit of two thousand million years, we shall be generous and say that Pioneer 10 will bump into alien clever dicks in a scant million years from now.

Folding evolution's Rorschach test back on the hinge of 1984, have you the remotest idea what Earthlings will look like in a million years' time, given how they were a million years back? Even if the Greenham Commoners are wrong and the handful of ennucleated survivors have not been mutated into polka-dotted gastropods with seventeen heads and a talking navel, are there not solid grounds for assuming that natural evolution will have taken a heavy toll of the NASA artist's impression? To cite the tiniest example: in Britain, the average height of a man over the past hundred years has risen by three inches. Do you have a calculator handy?

See?

I am not of course guaranteeing that our descendants in 1,000,1984 AD will all be 2500 feet tall, you can never tell about evolutionary roulette, some of them may be no taller than the Eiffel Tower, but whichever way you slice it, it is going to be extremely misleading to the things gathered round the wreck of Pioneer 10. Or take shape: glance again at the rather plump 1972 lady in the picture. Is she not unquestionably pre-diet-boom, pre-Fonda, pre-F-plan? Today, she would be twenty pounds slimmer; in a million years time, she could well be a thousand feet of thread, wound, perhaps, on a large reel for convenience, and living on amoebae.

Mind you, diet could well be a passing fad, just like employment: by 1,000,1984, such world as there is could be entirely run by robots, leaving the thousand-foot humanoids nothing to do but eat. Our grandchildren[10] may very well turn out to be fifty-ton lumps of suet, capable of nothing but rolling around and watching breakfast television.

If Warfarin-resistant rats haven't taken over, of course, or malathion-gobbling giant greenfly, grown huge and clever and nasty. The mutant options, the evolutionary permutations, the protoplastic swings and roundabouts are unimaginably limitless; compared with speculating about *them*, thinking of infinity is a doddle.

As for the odds on Pioneer 10 not heaving-to alongside something intelligent before the *further* end of its two-thousand-million-year manufacturer's warranty, the guesswork should not even be embarked upon without a doctor's certificate. We Earthlings could, by then, be itinerant warts, we could be chattering fungi, we could all be members of the Labour Party National Executive.

So, then, what might be the outcome of all this? The things from Planet X, beside themselves (unless, of course, they are already built that way) at the thought of intelligent life ten billion billion miles away, will hop/crawl/bounce/drip into their own spacecraft, and set out on the long trip Earthwards. A thousand million years later, and sick of tinned food, they will chuck open the hatch and hurl themselves onto the surface of this planet, gabbling:

'Take us to your leader! Where are the women with the big jugs?'

What will happen to this already battered old globe when they discover the truth, I dare not even begin to imagine. Regret at evolving beyond free-floating polymer blobs won't be the half of it.

Affluent Societies

Building societies are seeking wide-ranging extension of their powers. They wish to be permitted to operate banks and insurance companies, and to offer estate-agency and conveyancing services to the public. They also want permission to acquire land for housebuilding, and to lend for the purchase of consumer goods and second mortgages. In the report by the Building Societies Association, it was also emphasized that member-democracy should not be exercised at the expense of a society's efficiency. —Financial Times

IT WAS the scream that brought me out of my chair; but it was the bell that took me to the door.

There were two men on the mat. Shoulder-to-shoulder, they formed a camel-haired wall that blotted out the light. They had, apparently, been recently engaged in some form of strenuous exercise; their jaws shone like oiled slate.

'708/34a/672G?' snapped one.

'What?' I said.

They looked at one another. The slate shifted suddenly, like a satellite weather-map, as their cheek-muscles clenched.

'I don't believe he knows his number, Bingfax,' said one, quietly.

'I think you have put your finger on it there, Bradwich,' said the other. He sighed, and reached forward, unhurriedly; with a terrible finger and thumb, he plucked a button from my cardigan, and swallowed it. 'Members ought to remember their numbers,' he said.

'Members could get themselves into no end of trouble,' murmured Bradwich, 'forgetting their numbers.'

'There was a scream,' I said, tiptoeing to peer between their pulpy ears.

'Oh, there was,' said Bingfax. 'Definitely.'

'Ask us in,' said Bradwich. 'Politeness in members is something we are always on the lookout for, isn't it, Bingfax?'

'Definitely.' Bingfax removed his toothpick, wiped it on my sleeve, and placed it delicately in the brim of his fedora. 'Especially when it is our own house we are expecting to be invited into.'

I clapped my forehead! I sprang back!

'I *see*!' I cried. 'You are *that* Bradwich & Bingfax! Forgive me, gentlemen, I have never had a personal call from my building society before, I never imagined, I mean, to what do I owe this—'

'*His* building society,' muttered Bingfax, pushing past me into the hall and fingernailing a loose paint-flake from the dado. 'Do they never learn, Bradwich?'

'Do they buggery,' replied Bradwich. He turned off a radiator. 'You do not want to let our house get too warm, son,' he murmured. 'Could do untold damage to the fabric. Buckle joists, warp doors, attract mice, you name it. We could not answer for the consequences, could we, Bingfax?'

'Not entirely,' replied Bingfax. 'We could probably have a shrewd guess as to which of us would end up with a funny limp, but beyond that, we could not even begin to imagine.'

I looked at the radiator.

'It *is* the middle of winter,' I said, 'and, anyway, I do not see that it is any—'

'I do believe our member's cold,' said Bingfax. He gave me a little hug; a rib creaked; a bowel twanged. 'I do believe our member could do with a nice warm jacket.'

Bradwich took out a black leather notebook, and spat on his pencil.

'I shall put our member down for one of the new Bradfax Elite Gents hacking-jackets in thornproof tweedette,' he said. 'Centre vent, natural flare, very chic. Bottle-green, was it, or lovat?'

'I don't need a new jacket,' I said.

Bingfax sighed, and removed his hat, the better to bring his face down close to mine. He smelt of gun-oil.

'You do not want to go upsetting Mr Bradwich, son,' he said softly. 'Mr Bradwich was instrumental in setting-up our consumer-goods department. He could get very distressed at the thought of a member going around in a cardigan with half its bleeding buttons off. He would construe it as letting the society down, catch my drift? Also, under our wide-ranging new powers, anyone not ordering a natty Bradfax Elite spring outfit could have their mortgage took off 'em so bloody quick, their feet would not touch the ground. I would refer you to the small print.'

'I have read the small print!' I cried defiantly.

'Ah,' said Bingfax, 'but have you read the small print of the small print?'

'Personally,' said Bradwich, scribbling, 'I'd have the lovat. It will go with your new shoes and wallpaper.'

'Wallpaper?'

Bingfax glanced around, heavily.

'Do not think you are keeping this rubbish all over our walls,' he said. 'Not when there is Bingwich Elegant Flock on the market at £7.90 a roll.'

'Flock?' I cried. '*Flock?* This is not the bloody Doolalli Tandoori House!'

'It could be,' said Bradwich. 'We have not selected the new owner yet. Should he turn out to be some dusky entrepreneur willing to take out one of our Utensil-And-Crockery Second Business Mortgages, we shall not let prejudice stand in our way. He could be in here and pumping the vindaloo through the hatch before the ink's dry. Them little buggers do not let the grass grow, son.'

'But I'm not selling the house!' I cried.

''Course you're not,' replied Bingfax, soothingly. 'You are not qualified. Wichfax Real Estate will take all that off your hands, as stated in your mortgage agreement, that is partly why we are round here today, have a shufti, I trust you have kept the garden up, no black spot, mildew, thrips, all arris-rails made good as per specification, dog-droppings tidied, also guttering secure at all points, no birds-nests or tennis balls in same?'

'They may be black,' said Bradwich, 'but that don't mean they can't spot a blocked gulley, they could be off like a shot, you could be depriving the Bradwich & Bingfax of a firm sale, son, I wouldn't like to be in your shoes if that happened, family man are you?'

'He'd better be,' snapped Bingfax, 'I've got him down for two sons going to Faxwich College of Further Education next month, it's five grand a term there, he'd better not have sent in a false declaration on his mortgage form as to nature of family commitments!'

'I hope he's taking out a Special Lucky Bloody You Endowment Policy entitling him to considerable benefits in tax-concessions when linked to a recognized scheme for his children's education?'

'Yes,' said Bingfax, 'he is. It will form part of the codicil attached to his Stranger Things Have Happened Householders Policy offering him full protection in the event of his going down with the *Titanic* after they have raised it and it hits an iceberg again on its second maiden voyage.'

Bradwich looked at me.

'I didn't know you'd taken out one of them,' he said. 'You want to watch who you're keeping things from, as a member you have a responsibility to making sure the society is working at maximum efficiency. I could well have missed out an item of considerable benefit to your fellow members, i.e. if you're going on the *Titanic*, you'll need a full set of matching Faxbrad luggage. There was £178.40 plus VAT you were very nearly taking out of your fellow-members' mouths!'

I sat down. I licked cracked lips.

'Look,' I said, 'if I have to move—'

'Did he say if?' enquired Bradwich.

'Pretend you didn't hear him,' replied Bingfax. 'He's been with us fifteen years, he's entitled to the benefit of the doubt. Anyway, he hasn't signed our Private Patients Insurance Plan yet, we are not here to chuck money down the drain.'

'—where can I move to?'

'Erzanminefax Executive Homes!' they cried, together.

'Thought you'd never ask,' said Bradwich.

'It's a delightful estate of bijou residences designed with the mortgagee in mind,' said Bingfax. 'We are reclaiming the land this very minute. Normally, of course, we do not allow members to transfer their mortgages to anything on wheels with a communal khazi, but seeing as how you have been with

123

us fifteen years, we are prepared in your case to show magnanimity.'

'He may even get a choice of sink,' said Bradwich, 'mightn't he?'

'Steady!' cried Bingfax. 'We are not in this business for our health.'

Whereupon they snapped shut their notebooks, rebuttoned their overcoats, secured their hats, and turned towards the door. As they opened it a faint yet heart-rending groan echoed in.

'The scream!' I cried. 'I'd almost forgotten it. That must be the same person, I'll—'

'Bound to be,' said Bradwich. 'We do not muck about, son.'

'It is your next-door neighbour,' said Bingfax. 'Very difficult customer. He give us a lot of trouble, didn't he, Bradwich?'

'We had to break his thumbs,' replied Bradwich. 'Very nasty.'

'My God!' I shouted. 'There's been the most terrible mistake! I happen to know for a fact that he is not a member of the Bradwich & Bingfax Building Society!'

'He is now,' said Bradwich.

Animal Crackers

The family pet, whether a dog or cat, gerbil or goldfish, could save your life, claims an animal expert.
    Cambridge animal behaviourist Mr James Serpell says talking to pets can bring down high blood pressure and ease nervous tension.—
Daily Express

Dear Doctor Coren:
I hope you will not mind my writing to you, I could not help noticing the cutting you have just stuck at the top of your page and I thought you might want to hear my story with a view to putting in your two penn'orth, we must all love one another or die, as W. H. Auden said, an old fairy, true, but he knocked about a bit, as they do, of course, and he knew what was what, e.g., it's a funny old world we live in, but the world's not entirely to blame, and so forth.
    I did try contacting Mr James Serpell himself, but he kept putting the phone down, that is often the way it is with scientists, they say something, and you think to yourself, Hallo, that could be the answer, but when you open the paper the next day, no mention of it, it is just like *Tomorrow's World* on the telly, you see they have now come up with something, usually as the result of the space programme, that gets wine stains out of vests, only when you go round to Timothy White's or Robert Dyas they have never bloody heard of it, it is scientific irresponsibility of the worst kind, they just say the first thing that comes into their heads, scientists, and never mind the effect on the rest of us, look at that business with the black hole in the *Daily Mirror*, I gather it is eating galaxies left,

125

right and centre, it could be here by Tuesday for all I know, but you ring up people and ask, e.g. Citizen's Advice Bureau, Brian Hayes, etc., and do they tell you anything, do they bloody hell.

What I want to know is, is there anything in this business of talking to animals to, what is it, ease nervous tension? I only ask because I am quite a jumpy person, I don't know if that is what is meant by nervous tension, I keep going down my GP to ask him, but I cannot get a straight answer, could it be because he is a blackie, well, you do hear things, only now he has taken me off his, do they still call it a panel, anyway whatever it is I am off it, and being jumpy I do like to chat a bit, also very interested in the world and things about me, not just black holes but also how pebble-dash sticks to the walls and do all the sewers in England connect up or is it just sort of, you know, town-by-town, but I find that these days, people don't have time to listen, do you find that, Doctor Coren, do you, do you?

So I talk to the cat, but as soon as I sit it in the chair and open my mouth, it jumps up and it is behind the fridge before you can wink, and what I want to know is, if I could get it put down, e.g. gassed or run over by the vet or whatever it is they do, on the grounds that it was a bad listener, how would I go about getting a *good* listener, is there a place to advertise, is there a Nervous Tension And Cats Advisory Service you can ring, is there a special breed that like sitting there and listening, e.g. not Persian or Burmese, anything I said would be all gobbledegook, it would be behind the fridge in a flash, am I right?

Anyway, I look forward to your reply, by the way how high is high blood pressure, I tried that one on the blackie as well, but he looked at me as if I was mad.

Yours sincerely,
Alison Fermold.

Dear Doctor Coren:
I saw your name in the paper, and we are both men of the world, and since I have a small problem 'down there' which is preying on my mind a bit, I should like to know whether there is any point in telling my stick insect about it.

It is no fool, I have managed to get it to walk along a string, which is more than I could ever get my gyroscope to do, and it is able to disguise itself as several difficult things, e.g. a stick, a twig, a very thin log, but how can I be sure it is ready to cope with a somewhat tricky personal problem? I would feel a fool if I went into a long description and it went right over its head, and then again, there is the question of whether it would still respect me afterwards.

I really am at my wits' end, and I know my blood pressure is going up, there is this little vein in my temple which sort of lurches like a lugworm, and I have to talk to somebody. I have tried my stick insect on other subjects, such as the guttering coming away from the wall and the funny smell in my cap, and it looked quite interested, but this is a question of a different order.

Yours truly,
G. M. Denning

Dear Doctor Coren:
Can a cat keep its mouth shut?

I only ask because, as a person whose nervous tension is most frequently exacerbated by financial worries, I recently took the advice of your colleague Mr Serpell and confided in my cat, Derek, and, during the course of the conversation, inadvertently let slip my private account number at the Zurich Kreditanstalt. Derek did not register anything at the time, but that is often the way it is with cats, they are cunning little bastards.

In my opinion, the cat was acting professionally at the time and ought therefore to respect the normal ethics obtaining in a client-consultant relationship, in which case, if it chose to share this private information with other cats, I could presumably get if struck off whatever it is that cats are on. The thing is, how would I know?

Since, because of all this, my blood-pressure has gone even higher, would my best course be to confide in my dog, Dave, and hope that a nod would be as good as a wink, i.e. Dave would bite Derek's head off? In which case, should I rephrase the question, viz. Can a *dog* keep its mouth shut? I should not want to have to get Dave rubbed out, for one thing he is a big bugger and I would have to involve a lion, or something, for another he is pedigreed and stands in at around £250, and for a third, it is a bit academic whether a lion can keep its mouth shut or not since, apart from the practical difficulties involved, a respectable off-shore securities dealer who had a lion knee-capped could well find himself in dead trouble, that is just the kind of high-profile activity to get the Fraud Squad bastards reaching for their raincoats.

I do not know which way to turn. It is not easy, earning a living these days.

Yours faithfully,
Sir Eric Klutz

Dear Doctor Coren:

Does it matter whether a tortoise is in or out when you talk to it? Put another way, when it looks like a brick, do its ears still work?

I only ask because I recently discovered that my secretary was pregnant and, not knowing what action to take, I was a bit of a silly and put the problem to my tortoise.

I now realize it was shut at the time.

What I want to know is: did it hear anything?

I do not want to go through it all again, especially as I have now changed my mind about the matter, I think.

Yours truly,
(Name and address supplied)

Good Star, Bad Star

Relations between the Communist Party and the Morning Star *are set to reach crisis point soon in a purge which could topple the editor—* Sunday Times

THEY COME to me, and they said, well it is all stitched up, comrade, Konstantin Chernenko is the new proprietor, and he wants you to carry on as per usual, he would not dream of interfering in your editorial independence, just jot the name of next-of-kin on this little urn in the event of accidents, you never know with them high windows on the fourth floor, some of them have got very dodgy catches.

Konstantin Chernenko, I said, hasn't he just taken over *Pravda*, also Tass, plus I do not know how many top Warsaw Pact dailies, is that the same bloke?

Definitely, they replied, he is hot as effing mustard. He is a real big name in the media, we see it as a very exciting leap forward, and the *Morning Star* is one of his little favourites, it is a feather in his cap, big circulation nudging 16,000, genuine money-spinner, close on seventeen pound thirty when we opened the post yesterday, not to mention the prestige.

Well, I said, it is a big chance and no mistake, but I should have to seek certain safeguards.

Oh really, they said.

Not necessarily, I replied.

That's all right then, they said.

Will there be a board of independent national directors, I enquired, set up to guarantee the paper's integrity?

The new proprietor would not have it no other way, they affirmed. There are four of them in a smart room over the Elite Kebab Parlour, Farringdon Road, and they will be coming over here most days to open the post, change the leader column, and so forth. At the first sign of any integrity being buggered about with, they will make this place look like Scutari bloody Hospital. Does that meet with your editorial approval?

I am over the moon, I replied, this is the New Jerusalem. By the way, is Mr Chernenko worried about the attitude of the Monopolies Commission?

Not *worried* exactly, they said.

My staff were rather more, what's the word, cautious; especially the shorter one. This was largely out of loyalty to the former proprietor. Yuri Andropov was a newspaper tycoon of the old school. So long as you got on with the job, he left you alone. To my recollection, he never come down to Farringdon Road in all my years with the paper.

I hope this new bloke won't be hopping in and out every ten minutes, said the shorter one. As the Powder Keg Editor, I can affirm that this place is like a powder keg. All it would take is one spark. Look at El Salvador. Or, for instance, the Horn of thing, Africa.

Is something bothering you? I enquired.

He is worried about his hat peg, said the taller one. We both are. We have heard about Chernenko's whirlwind methods. As the Bloodsucking Entrepreneurial Shark Editor, I think I speak for all of us when I say we do not want some bloodsucking entrepreneurial shark coming in here without so much as a by-your-leave and putting his hat on our peg.

I fought for that hat peg, said the Powder Keg Editor. It was like Spain all over again. It was like the Ebro. I can remember putting in the original chitty: *one peg, wooden, hat, 3/6.* You wouldn't credit the barney up CP HQ. The place was like a powder keg. All it needed was one spark.

It was his great victory, said the Bloodsucking Entrepreneurial Shark Editor. It was his Stalingrad. He wouldn't want to go through all that again, just because of the devious entrepreneurial machinations of some bloody shark.

Such as who? I enquired.

Such as nobody, said the Powder Keg Editor. Who said

anything about anybody?

Certainly not me, said the Bloodsucking Entrepreneurial Shark Editor, definitely not me.

You would not be prepared to put up no editorial resistance to the Chernenko takeover then? I said.

He is one of nature's gentlemen, said the PKE; if he is a rough diamond, he is one of the best.

Exactly my point, agreed the BESE. I do not know what all the fuss is about, you would not catch me dead in a hat anyway, they make you go bald.

That night, I talked it all over with my lovely wife Tina, glittering spokescomrade of OVARIES AGAINST NATO and, as the heroperson responsible for bunging a brick through the window of the NUJ General Secretary in protest over their policy of discriminating against female illiterates, practically a journalist in her own right.

Her personal opinion was from each according to his abilities, to each according to his needs, i.e. who else was going to pay me close on thirty-one pound a week after stoppages, plus generous free bike-space on front railing and staff donor-card enabling my kidneys to help the great class struggle in the event of anyone at the embassy coming over a bit moby dick?

Also, I owed it to the paper. Was I not a great campaigning journalist who had fought for years against the iniquitously out-dated British electoral system which allowed honking prats from the gilded shires to maintain in office a Government able, by grinding the faces of the proletariat, to afford enough uniformed Fascists to withstand a democratic *coup d'état*? Was I not also a great news journalist who had scooped the entire British press with his story of how 99% of the Soviet people had too much to eat, which explained why the troops had not emerged from their tank-turrets to receive the roses hurled at them by the liberated Afghans, due to the danger of being stuck in same?

That is all true, I said, but are the new proprietor's assurances worth the paper they are written on?

What paper? she said.

It is just an expression, I said.

131

For the first few months, me and the proprietor got on like a palace on fire. Well, I say proprietor, I personally never saw hide nor hair of him, him being up Moscow and doubtless doing a dose-of-salts number on my *Pravda* comrade-colleagues etcetera, I do not know about that, the first rule of journalism is not to ask too many questions.

The people I did see were the Elite Kebab Parlour Four, i.e. the proprietor's legal representatives. They took to coming over of a morning and making sure we had the requisite number of references to lick-spittles, running dogs, astrakhan collars, warmongers, stooges, lies, neo-Nazis, slavering wolves, scum, and so forth, but we was normally up to snuff, so no problem there.

It was not until Monday, September 5, that the unthinkable happened.

I was just bending to take off my second bicycle clip, when I got this funny feeling that all was not as it should be. Call it a journalist's sixth sense. I straightened up, narrowed my eyes the way we are taught up the Northern Poly Investigative Reporters Course, and there it was!

An unidentified trilby was hanging on the Powder Keg Editor's Peg.

Oy, I shouted, pointing, what is that all about?

A chipboard door opened, revealing our lavvy and the four legal representatives standing round it. They appeared to my trained eye to be divvying up pound notes.

That is my hat, replied the legal firm's senior partner, a large man with a busted conk and the pulpy ears of a QC who has knocked about a bit. Why?

Oh, I said, well, I said, nothing much, it is just that you have inadvertently hung it on the Powder Keg Editor's peg. He might well construe that, comrade, as unwarranted interference in editorial affairs. I am not saying *I* would, I am saying *he* might, catch my drift?

They all come out of the khazi, after that, and looked at me.

Ask him, said the senior partner.

I immediately went into the PKE cubicle, and put the point.

As a matter of fact, said the Powder Keg Editor, I offered it to him voluntarily. Have my hat-peg, comrade, I said.

I looked at him for a long time.

You rotten treacherous little shitehawk, I said, comrade.

Are you referring to me, comrade? he replied, unabashed.

As one who spent many years on this paper as the official Treacherous Wall Street Shitehawk Editor, I replied, I know whereof I bleeding speak. Why have you stabbed me in the back?

It was his turn to look at me. He leaned back languidly in his executive kitchen chair, lit an opulent stub from the cocoa-tin on his desk, and said: I would give anything to be the Editor of the *Morning Star.* Wouldn't you?

I may have gone pale. Without replying, I turned, and strode back into the main office, intending to have it out there and then with the proprietor's representatives. I found them standing around the smart Tupperware box containing that morning's postal contributions for the Star Fund. I walked across, just in time to see one of the junior partners, a squat Slav in a new Cecil Gee karkoat, altering the cashbook carefully from £43.17 to £3.17.

This is a blatant falsification of our trading figures, I cried.

The squat Slav gazed at me.

So ask question in Kremlin, he said thickly. Wait for General Secretary's Question Time and ask Glorious People's General Secretary whether he has plans to visit Farringdon Road, heh-heh-heh!

I turned in supplication to the senior partner.

Perhaps, comrade, I said, there is a good reason for this. What is the money for?

It is for the Fighting Fund, he replied.

Who are you fighting? I enquired politely.

In answer, he bunched beneath my nose a fist the size and consistency of a wheel-chock.

Anybody we bleeding fancy, he said.

I looked across at the Bloodsucking Entrepreneurial Shark Editor, most loyal of all my crew.

Did you catch all that? I enquired.

Yes, he said, we took £3.17 in this morning, not bad at all, why are you so obsessed with money, you little bloodsucking entrepreneurial shark?

I gasped, and staggered back. There was a long silence. A cubicle door behind me opened.

This place is like a powder keg, said a voice. All it needs is one spark.

And that is about all there is to it. I asked the senior partner about severance, and he enquired as to which leg I would prefer. So I went downstairs, and I walked up Farringdon Road towards Fleet Street, knowing that I had done what had to be done, my whole mind and being obsessed with that one shining and imperishable thought with which the dedicated journalist meets, and ultimately conquers, Fate's crueller twists.

If I can get to a typewriter, I thought, there could well be a bob or two in this.

From Grave to Gay, by Turns, and Gay to Grave

The world's first funeral home staffed entirely by homosexuals and catering exclusively to the gay community has been opened in San Francisco by gay undertaker Tommy Simpson—Guardian

HAMLET

ACT V

Scene I. *A Churchyard. Enter two CLOWNS, with spades and pickaxes.*

FIRST CLOWN   So anyway, I gave him one of my looks, and—

SECOND CLOWN   One of your withering looks?

FIRST CLOWN   One of my withering looks, and I said: *Where is he?* And he said, in the car, and I said—I mean, I was shocked—

SECOND CLOWN   You would be.

FIRST CLOWN   —and I said, *in the boot?* I said, you haven't got your loved one in the *boot*, that is no way to treat the dear departed, I said, all scrunched up like a Waitrose turkey; apart from anything else, I said, he'll have gone rigid by now, we shall have to roll him into the shop, he'll get filthy, you do not, I take it, want your loved one covered in fag-ends and dog's doings, and if you think *I'm* carrying him in, I said, with *my* back, you've got another think coming, why didn't you leave

135

us to pick him up, I said, I could've sent Adrian and Siegfried with a selection of bespoke woods and we could've boxed him up on the premises, we spent a fortune on that hearse, I told him.

SECOND CLOWN   Good for you, Tristram. Some people!

FIRST CLOWN   Some people, Burt, *exactly*! Anyway, that's only the beginning, you won't believe what happened next, no sooner had—

SECOND CLOWN   Shall I put my spade down? You know me with my arms.

FIRST CLOWN   Yes, do, I can see that funny little sinew beginning to jump, it's making a mockery of your tattoo, I told you you should never have had a lily there, a lily's got to be in a calm place, you ought to have had a dragon, a dragon can take movement, you don't want a lily hopping about, especially with your skin. Where was I?

SECOND CLOWN   You were coming to what happened next.

FIRST CLOWN   Yes, well, what happened next was he said, no, I have not got him in the boot, I have got him in the front passenger seat, he said, but don't worry, he's got a seat belt on so he is not resting his forehead on the dashboard, I have got a reputation to keep up in this town, he said, he has gone a bit grey but no-one would clock him for a stiff.

SECOND CLOWN   *No*! Were those his exact words, Tristram?

FIRST CLOWN   They are embossed on my memory, Burt. *No-one would clock him for a stiff*!

SECOND CLOWN   You responded immediately, I take it?

FIRST CLOWN   Like a tiger, dear. You know me when my dander is up.

SECOND CLOWN   Frightening. Your whole mien changes, Tristram. Yours is not a dander to trifle with. Just talking about it has made your knuckles clench on your pick-handle, I can read H,A,L,L,O from right over here and I

136

	haven't even got my contacts in. So what did you say then?
FIRST CLOWN	I said *stiff*? Is that any way to talk about a loved one, I said, never mind strapping him in and bouncing him all over the place, do you realize how loved ones bruise after demise, I said, his botty will be like rotten plums.
SECOND CLOWN	You never!
FIRST CLOWN	Oh yes I did.
SECOND CLOWN	Did he break down? Did he sob?
FIRST CLOWN	Did he hell. He *laughed*.
SECOND CLOWN	I feel faint.
FIRST CLOWN	He laughed, Burt, and he said, *loved one*? he said, he's never a loved one, he's one off the boat, he said, I only met him last night, I think he's a Pole, possibly a Serb, he's got wooden dentures and psoriasis, I don't know about *your* taste, ducky, he said, but that is not my idea of a loved one, that is my idea of any port in a storm, nudge, nudge, catch my drift?
SECOND CLOWN	*Nudge, nudge, catch my drift?*
FIRST CLOWN	As I live and breathe.
SECOND CLOWN	I don't know what's happening to the gay community, Tristram, there used to be sensitivity, there used to be subtlety, there used to be *style*! All kinds of tat is coming out these days, where will it end?
FIRST CLOWN	I blame television. You wouldn't believe this one, he had a two-tone Escort with fluffy dice and a polystyrene Mannikin Pis with a diddly that lit up when he braked, he had a tattersall waistcoat with *all* the buttons done up and a bunch of keys sticking out of his top pocket, I very nearly told him to take his business elsewhere, there's such a thing as standards.
SECOND CLOWN	But your concern for the loved one prevailed?

FIRST CLOWN	You read me so well, Burt. Yes, you only had to look at our friend the tattersall waistcoat to realize that as far as the unfortunate loved one was concerned it was either a question of home is the sailor, home from the sea, courtesy of Ganymede Chic Interments Limited, or winding up in a lay-by on the A30 between a clapped-out Standard Vanguard and a rat-infested mattress. So Quentin and I brought him in.
SECOND CLOWN	It couldn't have been easy.
FIRST CLOWN	You don't know the half of it, dear. He was sat there stiff as a brick, we had to carry him in a fireman's lift, and we were half-way across the forecourt when this big butch constable suddenly appeared from behind our dwarf poplar!
SECOND CLOWN	*No!*
FIRST CLOWN	I don't know what might've happened without Quentin. He has marvellous presence of mind, for an ex-vintner. You know that roguish smile he has?
SECOND CLOWN	So well.
FIRST CLOWN	He just stopped, and turned that roguish smile on Mister Plod, and he said: Allo, allo, allo, there's never one around when *I* want one! Mister Plod did not know *where* to look!
SECOND CLOWN	Didn't he say anything about the loved one?
FIRST CLOWN	Oh, he mumbled something of the order of *what is all this ere*, the way they do, but you could tell his heart wasn't in it, and when Quentin said: *This? This is a cast of Rodin's Stoker, it's going on the Chief Constable's tomb*, he was off on his big chunky boots like something from the Dock Green *corps de ballet*.
SECOND CLOWN	Lucky you, Tristram.
FIRST CLOWN	Oh, really? You wouldn't say that if you'd been there, Burt, our troubles were only just

	beginning, we got the loved one inside, we hammered him straight, and then our tattersall friend turns round and says: Right! Can you do him in chipboard?
SECOND CLOWN	I would have scratched his eyes out. You know me.
FIRST CLOWN	Yes, you're not what I'd call managerial. *I* remained very calm.
SECOND CLOWN	Another withering look?
FIRST CLOWN	More sardonic, really. I gave him this sardonic look, and I said: Chipboard? *Chipboard?* This is Ganymede Chic Interments, I said, not bloody MFI! Why not cut your losses altogether, I said, Woolworth's do a very nice bin-liner for fifteen pee.
SECOND CLOWN	That was telling him, Trist!
FIRST CLOWN	So you might think, dear, so you might think, but just as I—hallo!

(*Enter HAMLET and HORATIO.*)

| HORATIO | Good morning, me and my friend would like to see a nice plot, the silly mare is thinking of doing away with himself, well, you know how the moody ones get sometimes, so I said I'd help him pick something out, he has absolutely no taste whatever, I don't think he's chosen a duvet cover in all the years I've known him, not that I think he'll go through with it, he can't make his bloody mind up from one day to the next, I don't know how I've stuck it all these . . . |

A Winter's Tale

(Being An Eleventh-Hour Entry for the Booker Prize)

Chapter One

It had been raining ever since Partition.

Each morning, my father would rise stiffly from his rude palliasse just inside the cane-door of our little *dhuni*, mix himself a poor breakfast of wind-dried rice and fish-head *ghosht* in his cracked wooden *numnah*, pad barefoot across the sodden rush-matting, stare out wretchedly towards the monsoon-veiled Kashmiri hills, and cry:

'For *this* we left Poland?'

Not unnaturally, the people of West Pakistan had not taken him to their hearts. A proud and embittered race who had suffered fearful depredation beneath the British vice-regal yoke—each spring, Edwina Mountbatten would descend upon the village like a tornado and carry off its young men—they were understandably suspicious of a Hassidic fenman in phylacteries and moleskin trousers who claimed to be writing a thesis on disputed kennings in *Beowulf*, and whose wife carried a self-loading Kalashnikov and a bonk-bag of hand grenades.

If anything, my mother Mgingi understood him even less. Brought up amid the unyielding scrub of the Namibian hinterland, her working knowledge of both Yiddish and Anglo-Saxon was scant, and to my father's obsessive hobby, the codification of eels, she brought nothing but a vague unease.

Structuralist readers will be enquiring as to exactly what it was that originally drew them together, to which I can only reply: misunderstanding.

Let me explain.

Chapter Two

Warsaw in the winter of 1942 was no place for a simple Lincolnshire ploughboy, drawn thither by an ambiguous article in *Freshwater Eel News.*

Determined to verify for himself a claimed sighting of Schmidt's elver in Lake Pyotzgw, my father seems to have encountered little difficulty in crossing occupied Europe, where, travelling the rural byways in his embroidered fenland smock and floral straw hat, and emitting only a high-pitched laugh to conceal his monolingualism, he was able to pass himself off as either the village idiot or the village gay.

When he finally crossed into Poland, however, his situation changed dramatically, and for the worse. In Poland, the village idiots had all been offered senior positions in the *Gauleiterei*, and wore brown three-piece suits, and the gays all wore SS uniforms, because that was where the really cute action was. The only people in round hats and caftans were Orthodox Jews.

My father, a sixteen-year-old who had hitherto experienced nothing more cosmopolitan than the Lincolnshire eel-ponds, could not, of course, grasp the nuances and implications of all this, and not unnaturally decided to pass himself off an an Orthodox Jew.

This was a mistake.

Chapter Three

Warsaw in the winter of 1942 was no place for a simple Namibian freedom fighter, drawn thither by the unparalleled opportunities for shooting Germans.

Her family's hatred of the Hun having matured during the years of the German protectorate of South-West Africa, my mother was given a further shot in the genes by the Afrikaaner's eager embrace of Nazism, and when, one sultry night, Marxist drums intimated to SWAPO HQ that anyone prepared to drop behind the Fascist lines and expunge the beastliness at source would be given a free submachine-gun and two dozen clips, she immediately filled her douche-bag with *biltong* and headed north.

It took her two years, soon to be a major movie. She reached the Mediterranean coast of Egypt on October 26, 1942, three days after El Alamein, and, by singing 'Lilli Marlene' in a series of waterfront *estaminets*, finally managed to persuade the British authorities that she was Ella Fitzgerald, sent on in advance by Roosevelt to soften up audiences for Larry Adler. Her next booking, she said, was the Russian front, but it was all pretty hush-hush, and a susceptible flight-lieutenant was persuaded to smuggle her aboard a Blenheim, from which, on the moonless night of November 3, she parachuted into Poland.

The whole place was white.

It was an experience entirely alien to her. Thus, her first victim on enemy soil was a short fat man clad only in an old muffler and a battered trilby, who stared fixedly at her from little black eyes. She threw a karate chop, and his head came off.

It felt good.

The Nazis were going to be a pushover.

Chapter Four

For two long years, my father and his small group of itinerant rabbinical students kept one step ahead of the Nazis.

Hidden deep in the Carpathian forests, my father worked hard at his Hebrew, trying to discover the word for *eel*. None of the others would help him, fearing that as soon as he learned it, he would be off in search of Lake Pyotzgw, leaving a trail which might well lead back to them.

And then, when all seemed well-nigh lost, Fate entered these ravelled lists!

On a keen January morning in 1945, as the fragmented German forces were flushed from their final covers, a small band of Polish partisans broke through and relieved my father's beleaguered party. They were led by my mother, whom the Polish resistance, never having set eyes on an African woman before, had taken to be a British commando, blacked-up for camouflage purposes. They had followed her everywhere, out of blind loyalty and faith. Many believed she was a Churchill. Under her direction, they had during the foregoing two years done everything from digging for yams to shooting anyone in an old muffler and a battered trilby, convinced by my mother that this was what identified a Wehrmacht officer.

Their devotion, in fact, was to be their subsequent undoing. Having all learned Afrikaans, under the impression that it was English, several of them later ran forward to meet an advanced patrol of the American 8th Airborne, who, taking the shouted greetings to be German, defiance, shot them in their tracks.

Of such ironies is war, and indeed contemporary fiction, made.

For the Hassidim, now that the war was virtually over, they went into a long discussion and finally agreed to tell my father not only the word for *eel*, but also the quickest route to Lake Pyotzgw. That night, he set off to find it.

My mother Mgingi, for reasons which will soon be made clear, followed him.

Chapter Five

Schmidt's elver was nowhere to be found.

Elsewhere in Europe, while Hitler's best man struggled to find the ring, while Vera Lynn danced in the Trafalgar Square fountains, while ATS princesses like Elizabeth and Margaret queued for their demob suits, my father waded Lake Pyotzgw with his makeshift net and my mother machine-gunned migrating geese to keep her hand in.

Eventually, my father splashed ashore and said:

'You spend three years looking for eels and what do you get? Heartache you get.'

Of the Lincolnshire burr there was now no trace.

'Marry me,' said my mother, in Afrikaans.

He stared at her, uncomprehendingly.

Chapter Six

Mgingi's thinking was this: she now did not wish to return to

143

Namibia. She liked Poland; she had grown fond of snow, and there was so much to shoot. If she went back to Namibia, she would have to give up the gun. The only way to stay in Poland was to marry a Pole.

Oddly, my father had begun to proceed along not altogether dissimilar lines. Having catalogued all the eel-types of England, he no longer had any interest in returning. He wanted to go to America, which had more eel varieties than anywhere else, but the only way to buck the post-war US immigrant quota system was to marry an American.

One night, as they lay camped beside the Pyotzgw-Lodz road on their way back from the lake, my father, unable to sleep, began going through my mother's knapsack. It was then that he found, fingers trembling, the *laissez-passer* signed by the British authorities in Egypt to the effect that my mother was Ella Fitzgerald, much-loved singer of the ever-popular 'Lilli Marlene', now bound for the Russian front.

Why my mother should have assumed the identity of a gobbledegook-speaking British commando, my father neither asked himself nor cared. Probably, he felt that that was what undercover agents behind German lines did.

As soon as she woke up, he grasped her shoulder, eyes blazing.

'Marry me,' said my father, in English.

She stared at him, uncomprehendingly.

Chapter Seven

A week later, in Soviet-occupied Warsaw, my mother was greeted as a Glorious People's Heroine, and nothing was too good for her. Having made their nuptial wishes known, separately, to the authorities, my parents were married in the flower-bedecked turret of a burnt-out Tiger by no less a figure than a weeping Red Army general.

For two days they were blissfully happy, each working on his and her private future plans. It was only when they approached the Allied Care & Rehabilitation officer, a man bilingual in English and Afrikaans, hoping to clear up the minor details, that the awful truth was made known to them.

144

However, after a short but lively encounter in which the office was wrecked, my father's eel-pole broken, and my mother's gun-butt badly scored by my father's front teeth, the C & R Officer, trained to handle such tragic cases, came up with a solution. Since they could neither stay in Poland nor emigrate to America, and since neither had any desire to return either to England or Namibia, had they, he enquired, considered a Malcolm Bradbury Travelling Fellowship?

'What's that?' asked my father.

'A MBTF,' said the C & R Officer, 'enables the holder to reside in the underprivileged country of his choice for as long as it takes him to collect enough material to write a satirical novel about it. Generous living expenses are paid by the underprivileged country's government.'

'I'll take two,' said my father, 'where do I sign?'

'You have to take a thesis subject,' said the Officer, 'just for appearance's sake.'

'Eels,' snapped my father instantly.

The officer licked his finger and ran it down a typed column.

'No good,' he said finally, 'two novelists and a blank-verse playwright have taken all three eel theses. How about disputed kennings in *Beowulf*? Always a winner, that.'

'Done!' cried my father.

On May 30, 1945, my parents sailed for what was then India.

Chapter Eight

I was born in March, 1946. For the past thirty-seven years, I have been carefully storing material about the foregoing items, in the hope that I may one day turn them into a really major modern cheque.

But every year, before I can finish, somebody else grabs one or other of my themes and beats me to it.

This year, I have figured out a way to see them all off. The main trouble is, I only just worked out how, which means the book has come out a bit short.

Still, as my father would say, is that so terrible?

Going By The Book

Radical changes in Metropolitan Police prosecuting policy will lead to a drop in cases brought to court and an increase in cautions.

Chief Inspector Brian Plaxton, the Scotland Yard officer in charge of implementing the new policy, told the Observer that he felt it was 'a more fair and compassionate one'.

'It will require every London police officer to be something of a sociologist,' he said.—Observer

EVENING ALL!

Well, that about wraps it up for another week. You're probably all wondering about the baffling case involving old Mrs Cotteslowe the sub-postmistress and the housebrick, and I'm glad to say we solved that little number to everybody's satisfaction. Turned out to be none other than our old friend, territorial distribution! The Super consulted P. M. Hauser and O. D. Duncan, *The Study of Population: an Inventory and Appraisal*, University of Chicago, 1959, and it was quite clear that young Brian had hit Mrs Cotteslowe with the brick due to her walking over the paving-stone he was about to spit on. It should have been obvious to PC Wilkes or any other student of urban demography, but there you are—in this job, a clue can be staring you right in the face and you never notice it! It's my guess as how he was led off the scent by her being a sub-postmistress, thus leading to the hurried conclusion that what young Brian was actually doing was rejecting the notional State as represented by a symbol of the State's vested authority (William Kornhauser, *The Politics of Mass Society*, 1959), something that can easily happen to an F-category urban, especially when he has got a conkful of Evostick and thinks he is Rudolf Hess.

146

'Course, territorial distribution does not entirely explain the phenomenon of him nicking her handbag contents, to wit £32.40, and there has been a bit of the usual argy-bargy between CID and Uniformed over this, I don't mind saying! CID reckon it is down to an attempt to eradicate what Dahrendorf identifies as the Prestige And Income Differentiation (*On the Origin of Inequality among Men*, Stanford University, 1958), whereas the uniformed branch feel that it was done in response to an Impositional Pattern, i.e., if you drew a graph, you would see the little sod has eighty-eight previous convictions.

Anyway, all's well that ends well: we apologized to young Brian for keeping him hanging about half the morning, and we sent him off with a book token to W. H. Smith by way of compensation. An hour or two with T. H. Marshall's *Class Conflict and Social Stratification* should sort him out double-quick.

As to the peculiar incident of the lead-stripping off of St Swithin's, we ended up having to hand *that* little item over to the Serious Sociology Squad! We thought we had Chummy and his oppo bang to rights, pair of jobless lapsed Episcopalians, *one a former choirboy, the other one ex-SAS*, it was as clear a case of aggravated protest in a post-Christian society as we have ever come across down Dock Green, especially given the infrastratal factor of the SAS indicant pointing to a personality *sanctioned* to operate ex-legally, thus anti-socially.

Shows you how wrong you can be! We got Chummy down the nick and allowed him his one call to his sociologist, and it was only a disciple of A. H. bloody Hawley, wasn't it? Naturally, we had all read *Human Ecology*, it is basic wossname up Hendon Police College, but we had never applied the principle of collective adaptation to a case of lead-stripping. Don't ask me why, but there it is. According to Chummy's sociologist, they was up on the roof in an attempt to restructure the community environment to suit altered needs, i.e. St Swithin's is only used for bingo these days, and if rain comes through the roof the old dears won't notice on account of they never take their plastic rainhoods off anyway.

'This is a bloody hot one, all right!' says the Super. 'I am getting this little number out of our hair bloody sharp, this is not a local nick parameter in any way, shape or form!'

147

Last I heard, the Serious Sociology lads were running R. F. Wessalowski's Disintegration Tables through the police computer: don't ask me why, it is not my field, but I *have* heard, on the old grapevine, that it's got something to do with the fact that the minivan that Chummy and his little friend used to cart all the lead away in had dodgy plates.

I know a lot of you who were left in suspense at the end of last week's episode will want to know whether we managed to clear up the unfortunate strangling of Mrs Eulalia Garsmold by her husband Clyde. Naturally, since she had been having it away with the gas-man, the rent-man, the window-cleaner, and a couple of blokes who had pressed the wrong bell, everything pointed to her husband having improperly adjusted to the fact that the Council have just replaced the trees outside their flat with street lamps. According to G. W. Blacklock's *Nochi Kaikaku: Some Studies of Greenbelt Loss in Suburban Kyoto*, urban aggression often rises in direct ratio to the systematic destruction of the natural environment (cf. also *The Failure of Crypto-Ruralism: Sexual Deviation in Welwyn Garden City*, Holt and Diderich, 1963, for some fascinating, what's the bloody word, analogues).

We could not have been further from the mark! Forensic was just photographing the new street-lamps and we were putting the finishing touches to our on-site reports, when young PC Phillips suddenly turns to me and he says: 'Hang about, Sarge, is it just me, or what?'

I looked at him. He is no more than twenty, just scraped home in his Anthropology A-level, but sharp for all that.

'What is it, son?' I said.

'There's something missing,' he replied, 'unless I am very much mistaken.'

We all looked at him, this time.

'Missing?' says the Inspector.

'There's no little corner shop,' says Phillips.

We walked into the middle of the road, examining both sides.

'Bloody hellfire!' muttered the Inspector. 'He's right!'

'Stone me!' I said. 'Tower block, no little corner shop, that can mean only one thing . . .'

'Right!' cried the Inspector. 'Forget the bloody street-lamps, they are merely an ancillary symptom, what we have got here, lads, is nothing less that a case of . . .'

'. . . a deracinated community!' we all shouted.

The Inspector nodded.

'The environment has been sociorationalized,' he said quietly. 'That poor bastard Clyde Garsmold never stood a chance. I wouldn't mind betting—it's just a hunch, of course—I wouldn't mind betting there used to be a pub here, too.'

I whistled.

'Do you think they had outside bogs, Inspector,' I said, 'where they would frequently run into one another and enjoy social interface?'

'Hard to say, lad,' he replied, 'but in a case like this, anything's possible.'

Well, naturally, in the light of this astonishing new evidence, we did not press charges. There is not a court in the country what would hold a man responsible for his actions after his entire environment had been ruthlessly restructured to serve an econopolitical nexus totally unconcerned with the sociopsychological consequences. Ask anyone on the beat.

Anyway, time I was off. I got this very tricky little case to sort out, heartbreaking really, bloke found himself with three hundred thousand quidsworth of stuff on his hands. He's been going round stately homes as a dialectical materialist, and he can't get in his drum for bloody candelabra. So I've offered to fence it for him, it's the least I can do.

And, yes, in case you were wondering, he is bunging me ten grand for my pains, but it is all right, I have got a clearance. I informed the Super and he said not to worry, nobody in his right mind would interpret it as being on the take.

It was more of a cry for help, really.

Fish Out of Water

The Chertsey man who landed the first salmon to be hooked in the Thames for 150 years said yesterday: 'It was nothing. The fish was knackered. He came quietly—there was no struggle.'—Daily Telegraph

THE SALMON, feeling good, feeling fit, turned sharp west at Margate, jinked nimbly past a sinking beer-can, and hit the estuary at a lively clip, humming to itself as only salmon can.

'Good holiday?' said a mackerel.

'Terrific,' said the salmon. 'Great. You cannot top the North Sea in August, I have been about a bit and I speak as one who knows.'

'Oh, I don't know,' said the mackerel, not without the smugness of its race, 'it's been pretty good in England, this year.'

The salmon fixed it with one penetrating eye, while the other kept circumspect watch on a gently descending turd.

'Oh, really?' it said.

'Definitely,' replied the mackerel, firmly. 'Anyone going abroad this year was bloody barmy. It has been,' and here he tapped the salmon with an emphatic fin, 'the best summer since records were thing, collected. Phew, what a scorcher, cried millions of holidaymakers as they made for the coast in droves, seeking relief from the boiling sun.'

'I fail to see,' said the salmon, 'how that could make any possible difference, down here.'

'You wouldn't,' said the mackerel, 'not having been here. Having made the mistake of going away, as it were. Would he?'

This last was addressed to a passing eel, who turned, at least in part.

150

'Would he what?' said the eel.

'Know how good it's been down here,' said the mackerel, 'if he's been up the North Sea.'

'Mad, going off,' confirmed the eel. 'All these holidaymakers, all these packed boatrides, you wouldn't credit the stuff floating down. I've been on cheeseburgers for two months solid.'

'See?' said the mackerel, triumphantly.

'You can get choc-ices,' added the eel, 'if you're nippy. Got a tendency to melt in the warm water, if you're not quick off the mark, but you soon pick up the knack.'

A burst of bubbles exploded from the salmon's mouth.

'Half-eaten cheeseburgers?' it cried. 'Soggy Cornettos?'

'Cornett*i*,' corrected the eel, 'strictly speaking. I would have thought you would have known that,' it continued nastily, 'being a traveller.'

'Yes, well,' said the salmon, 'you know what you can do with all *that* muck! You cannot beat foreign food, you would not credit what they lay on up the North Sea, juicy little sprats, nice fat plankton, and they've got a way with whitebait you just wouldn't—'

'You can get all that stuff here,' sneered the mackerel, 'if you know where to look. There's plenty of places in England that do that foreign rubbish—*and* do it better. I could mention a dozen. Not that I'd touch it, personally.'

'Goes right through you,' nodded the eel, 'whitebait. I went half-way across the Channel once, I was ill for days.'

The salmon glared at them, hard, clenched its little teeth, flicked its powerful tail, and shot away up river. Welcome home, it thought.

By Sheerness, however, it had regained most of its sense of well-being. A skate, cruising the frontier of acceptable salinity, glided past.

'Off home, then?' it said.

'Right,' replied the salmon.

The skate braked, and hove to alongside, leering.

'Come back home for a bit of the other?' it cackled. 'After a bit of the old domestic fin-over, are we?'

The salmon looked at it.

'I'm a salmon,' it said. 'It's what I do. Every summer I go off to feed, then I come back up-river to spawn. That is the name of the game.'

'Get off!' cried the skate. 'Pull this one!'

'Which one?'

'It's just an expression,' said the skate. It paddled around, with a neat little flick, to face the salmon head-on. 'Are you seriously telling me that if there was good stuff up the North Sea, you'd be belting back here? It is what I have always maintained, everybody rushing off abroad for the nooky, only when they get there, it is all rubbish. Either that or they do not fancy it, due to strict upbringing, etcetera. You cannot kid me, sunshine! Come on, fish-to-fish, straight up—did you get any?'

There was a long silence. Far above, a tug hooted.

'It is not why I went,' said the salmon, at last.

'Oh, really?' mocked the skate. 'Oh, well, pardon me, I'm sure, and here was I thinking: poor bugger, every year he trogs off for a touch of your oo-la-la, every year he comes running back to where the good stuff is, well, well, well, just shows you how wrong you can be, stone me, who'd have credited . . .'

And it swam languidly away, derisive laughter bursting from each trailing bubble. The salmon stared after it; eased slowly from bitterness to resignation; and pushed on, gloomily.

'North Sea again, was it?' enquired a pockmarked gudgeon off Gravesend.

'Yes,' replied the salmon, 'and in case you were wondering, I had a really fantastic eight . . .'

'Nothing to do in the evenings, is there?' said the gudgeon. 'As I understand it, the North Sea is bloody dead after six o'clock.'

The salmon chewed its little lip, and breathed in, deeply.

'Have you been recently?' it murmured.

'Me?' enquired the gudgeon. '*Me*? I wouldn't be caught dead up the North Sea! Well,' and here it laughed unpleasantly, 'as a matter of fact that is exactly what I would be. Caught dead. All that salt. I don't know how you *stand* that climate, you're bloody lucky not to end up pickled, no doubt you are currently congratulating yourself on getting back to dear old England in the nick of time?'

'I am a salmon,' snapped the homecomer, 'you ignorant little nerd! I am a sophisticated bleeding international

152

globetrotter, I am equally at home in fresh, salt, or brackish, you name it, I *love* the sea!'

The gudgeon nodded.

'Yes, you'd have to say that, of course,' it said. 'Going back to the same foreign dump year after year, you'd have to say you liked it or people'd think you needed your head looking at. I quite understand, mate.'

Whereupon it deftly doged the salmon's cumbrous lunge, and skittered away into the enfolding weed.

Is it worth going on? I ask myself, the salmon asked itself.

But it went on, because it was a salmon, and there was nothing else it could do.

'Bring anything back?' called a minnow, off Woolwich. And, without waiting for a reply, continued: 'No, well, you wouldn't really, would you, there's bugger-all there, load of tatty foreign junk, falls to bits on the trip home, I've heard about that, not worth bothering about, must be nice to be back.'

But the salmon did not even pause to reply, nor indeed to think about whether it cared or not, since it was fairly rapidly ceasing to care about anything much. It swam slowly and moodily on, feeling not just the benefits but the very memory of its holiday seep out of its homecoming scales. It passed wearily through the Pool of London, rolled with the sluggish tide through Chelsea Reach, and was just coasting past Fulham when, through what had gradually become a depressed reverie, it heard the faint but penetrating voice of a roach.

'Back off holiday?' enquired the tiny fish, circling the salmon.

The salmon ignored it.

'Dogger Bank again, was it?' persisted the roach.

The salmon slowed, and set its imperceptible jaw.

'Don't bother,' it muttered. 'It has already been borne in upon me what a prat I have been in going away. I have already been reliably informed what a marvellous bloody country this is. Better fish than you have already dinned into me the fact that I am over the moon to be home, and what a lucky bastard I am. Thank you very much.'

'I wouldn't say that,' said the roach. 'In fact, it is my considered view, as a roach, that you are a mug to *come* back.'

The salmon backfinned itself to a stop, and cast an eye roachwards.

'What?' it said.

'Where you from?' replied the roach obliquely. 'Where's you know, home?'

'Chertsey,' said the salmon. 'Chertsey is where the family is. Where I start it, anyway,' it amplified. 'Why?'

'Very nice, Chertsey,' said the roach. 'Very smart. Very secluded. Beats me how you find it every year.'

'Trade secret,' said the salmon. 'You have to be a salmon. Being a salmon is the only method of getting from the North Sea to Chertsey, take my word.'

'I believe you,' said the roach. 'You poor sod,' it added.

'I'm sorry?' enquired the salmon.

'Not only very smart,' murmured the roach, almost to itself, 'it is also very clean, Chertsey. You can see your face in it.'

'It is one of its strong points,' acknowledged the salmon.

'Oh,' said the roach, 'is it? Is it really?'

The salmon stared at the roach for a while, holding itself motionless against the running tide.

'Is there something I should know?' it enquired finally.

'It wouldn't make any odds,' answered the roach. 'There is no way of stopping you from going to Chertsey, is there?'

'I am a salmon. There is this inexorable urge.'

'Yes,' nodded the roach, 'there would be.'

And it shot off, leaving the bewildered salmon even more wretched than before. So it gave in to the rhythm of its old genetic song, and swam wearily on, as the Thames grew ever narrower and ever cleaner, and it dragged itself at last under the shadow of Chertsey Bridge, and it thought to itself, miserably: *it is as if I had never been away.*

But it wasn't.

It had never seen a line before, but by some buried atavistic blip, the salmon recognized it. It's always the way, it thought tiredly, you come back off holiday and something's gone wrong with the place. A thousand miles to the North Sea, it reflected, a thousand miles back, what is it all for, why do we bloody bother?

God, it thought, I'm knackered.

And, not ungratefully, it took the hook.

154

£10.66 And All That

A Dorset wood which was valued at £9 in the Domesday Book is now on the market at £120,000 — Daily Telegraph

GLOOMILY, THE Shaftesbury branch-manager of William & Bastards rubbed a clear patch in the little mullioned window with his smocked elbow, and stared out.

'Cats and dogs,' he muttered.

'What?' said his assistant.

'The rain is coming down,' replied the manager, 'cats and dogs.'

'Bloody portent, that is,' said the assistant. 'There'll be bishops dead all over by tea-time.'

'Not *real* cats and dogs,' said the manager, irritably. 'It is just an expression.'

'It doesn't mean anything,' said his assistant.

The manager rolled his eyes, rooted in his hirsute ear, cracked a hidden nit.

'You cannot expect to know what everything means, these days,' he said. 'The language is in a state of flux. Cats and dogs is probably from the Norman.'

'Why not?' grumbled the assistant. 'Everything else bloody is. I never eat out any more. Time was, you found a maggot on your plate, you stuck an axe in the cook. These days it's more than likely simmered in a cream sauce with a bloody peppercorn on its head.'

The manager sighed.

'Nevertheless,' he said, 'estate agency is nothing if not adaptable to change. We are at the forefront, Egwyne. We have got to be perceived to be red-hot. Hence smart fashionable expressions, e.g. cats and dogs.'

155

'What is e.g. when it's at home?' enquired the assistant.

'It's another one,' replied the manager. 'You hear it everywher.' He peered out again. 'Funny thing about this glass stuff,' he said, 'it makes people's legs go little. That woman from Number Four just went past, her feet were coming out of her knees. Her dog looked more like a bloody lizard.'

'If she finds out it's the glass what's doing it,' said the assistant, 'she could very likely sue us. I reckon we ought to have it took out again, God knows what it's doing to our eyes, they could start going little any minute, why did we have it put in in the first place?'

'It is what is called chic,' said the manager.

His assistant stared at him.

'Do not blame me, Egwyne,' said the manager, looking away, 'this stuff is coming straight down from head office. I am getting memos headed *From the Stool Of The Senior Bastard* informing me they are determined to drag estate agency into the eleventh century. You do not know the half of it, Egwyne. It is a whole new, er, ball game. It is where it's at.'

His assistant sniffed.

'I wouldn't care,' he said, 'we've hardly shifted nothing since we were set up. It may well be estate agency is not a British thing.'

'Concept.'

'What?'

'Never mind. Since you raise the point, Egwyne, the plain fact is it is all a matter of marketing.'

'What is marketing?'

'It is the name of the game. The old days of if you want somewhere to live you go round to the bloke with three chickens and if he doesn't reckon it's a fair price you knock him about a bit are over, Egwyne.'

The shop-bell tinkled. A young couple, entering, shrieked and ran out again. The manager hurried to the open doorway.

'What is it?' cried the young man, backing off. 'Leprosy? Boils? Ague?'

'Do not be alarmed!' replied the manager. 'It is only a concept. It rings when you open the door.'

His assistant appeared at his shoulder.

156

'Yes,' he said reassuringly, 'it is a ball game where it's at. Come on in out of the cats and dogs, it's bloody chic in here, e.g.'

Hesitantly, the young couple re-entered.

'We're after a hut,' said the man.

The manager beamed, drew up a pair of stools, flicked an unidentified dropping from one, and motioned his clients seated.

'And what sort of price range are we talking about?' he said.

'About eight bob,' said the husband, 'tops.'

The manager sucked his teeth.

'What have we got in the way of eight-bob huts, Egwyne?' he said.

'There's that rat-riddled old drum we've been trying to shift down by Aelfthryth's Swamp,' said his assistant, 'or possibly in it, by now; you know what it's like with bogs.'

'Rats?' enquired the young woman.

'Not large ones,' said the manager. 'Some of 'em are virtually mice. It's got a lot of roof.'

'It would have to have,' said the young man, 'for eight bob.'

'I'm not saying eight bob,' said the manager, quickly. 'We could certainly knock one-and-threepence off for cash. It's got a door up one end with a brand new string on it,' he added, 'it's got a ladder for climbing up to repair some of the roof it hasn't got, and a nice window without any of that glass what makes your legs shrink.'

'Has it got a floor?' enquired the young man.

'All right, six bob,' said the manager.

'Any land?' aid the young man.

'Ah,' said the manager. 'It has got land, hasn't it, Egwyne?'

'No point denying it,' said his assistant. 'They'd notice it straight away, anyhow. You cannot miss it, bloody great forest out back, could be anything in there, goblins, bogeys, trolls, you name it, well, it wouldn't be five bob otherwise, would it?'

'Four and sevenpence,' said the manager. 'It's got a relatively scum-free well, mind.'

'I don't know,' said the young woman, 'we were rather set on . . .'

'Tell you what,' said the manager quickly, 'you could chop the trees down, anything nasty'd soon run out, call it four bob

and I'll chuck in Egwyne to come round with his axe, he'll
have that lot down in next to no—'

But the shop bell had tinkled again. Egwyne watched them
go, from the window.

'She'll never fancy him now his legs have gone little,' he
said. He grinned. 'Serve 'em right, it was a steal at four bob,
some people don't know when they're lucky.'

The manager might well have responded, had not the door
opened again.

It was a slim young man in a neatly tailored smock, flared,
patch pockets, and polychrome embroidery at the scalloped
neck. He was clean-shaven, save for a thread of ginger
moustache, astonishingly symmetrical for the period, and his
hair glinted with polished lard. He had at least four teeth.

'Good morning,' he said. 'Edward the Smart, from head
office.'

The manager and his assistant cringed expertly backwards.

'Sir,' they murmured, 'sir.'

Edward the Smart waved the deference away with one
heavily ringed hand, while the other raised a large leather-
bound book it had been holding and laid it on their table.

'We have noticed up head office,' he said, 'that Shaftesbury
is into a disappointing situation tradewise. In short, as of this
moment in time, you have shifted sod-all.'

'It is always a bit quiet after a war, Edward the Smart, sir,'
mumbled the manager. 'People want to be dead sure the
pillaging etcetera has finished before rushing into property.'

'E.g.,' added his assistant, keenly.

'Yes, well, be that as it may,' said the man from head office,
'we have something we wish for you to run up the flagpole.'

The manager narrowed his imperceptible brows.

'Is it a concept?' he asked. 'Is it red-hot and chic?'

Edward the Smart looked at him, and knuckled his
moustache smooth.

'It is called advertising,' he said. 'We have just invented it.'

'Is it like cream sauce?' enquired the assistant, eager to
commend himself. 'Is it like snails' legs? Is it e.g.?'

Edward the Smart opened the big book. The page was
blank.

'This is what we call the *Domesday Book*. It is a property

guide. It goes free to everybody earning more than two pounds per annum.'

'The rich get everything,' muttered Egwyne.

'On each page,' continued the man from head office, 'William & Bastards will advertise a desirable property to the discerning buyer. Now, what can we put in from the Shaftesbury branch?'

'We got a four-bob rat-infested drum in the middle of a haunted wood,' said the manager. 'That's about it.'

'Better write down three-and-six,' said his assistant. 'No point misleading anybody.'

Edward the Smart looked at him for a very long time. Finally he said:

'Do you have a written specification of this item?'

The manager produced a crumpled note, licked a cheese-crumb off it, and handed it across. Edward the Smart considered it for a while, hummed a snatch or two of galliard, finally began to write.

'Just in the market,' he said aloud, quill darting, 'a bijou cottage-style residence in the midst of a fine wooded country estate, magnificently located beside a lush water-meadow supporting a truly rich profusion of wild life. The house itself is wholly original and constructed from local materials to blend perfectly with its environment, and requires only a touch of sympathetic decoration to create a magnificent rural retreat that is, nevertheless, being secluded but not isolated, within easy reach of all amenities. The superb woods which go with the property are rich in local legend, and offer a mature aspect from all windows. Due to bereavement, the present titled owners wish to dispose of the property quickly, a factor reflected by the realistic price of only nine pounds. An early inspection is advised.'

Edward the Smart put down his quill.

The manager was whimpering quietly in the corner.

The assistant licked dry lips.

'Nine pounds?' he croaked, finally, '*nine pounds?*'

Edward the Smart snapped shut his book.

'Yes, I know what you're going to say,' he said, 'but if it *does* turn out to be underpriced and we get a few nibbles, we can always withdraw it, bung it in at auction, and crank it up a bit on the day, could go as high as a tenner. I take it you have a false beard and something to wave?'

And with that, he was gone.

Slowly, the manager pulled himself together and hobbled to the window.

'Tell you a funny thing,' he said, 'his legs haven't gone little. What do you suppose that means?'

The assistant thought for a while.

'That he's Old Nick?' he said.

'E.g.,' replied the manager.